Propaganda
and
Psychological Warfare

STUDIES IN
POLITICAL
SCIENCE

Propaganda
and
Psychological Warfare

by

TERENCE H. QUALTER

University of Waterloo

RANDOM HOUSE • NEW YORK

TO

H. R. G. Greaves

LONDON SCHOOL OF ECONOMICS

Preface

This book originated from a doctoral thesis, *The Nature of Propaganda and Its Function on Democratic Government: An Examination of the Principal Theories of Propaganda Since 1880,* submitted at the University of London in 1956. Apart from the chapter on "The Theory of Propaganda," however, it now bears very little relation to that thesis. Most of the material is new and covers topics not originally dealt with at all. Some of the present argument first appeared in the author's article, "The Manipulation of Popular Impulse," (*Canadian Journal of Economics and Political Science,* XXV (1959).

Contents

Introduction

The specter of the omnipotent but amoral propagandist now haunts the educated and semi-educated strata of society.[1]

What might this instrument of measureless blackmail and most shameful humiliation not have become in the hands of a government mindful to whip up national passions to boiling point! How might propaganda of genius not turned to account its sadistic cruelties in order to transform the indifference of the people into indignation, and its indignation into hottest rage. . . . But to do this everything from child's story-book to the last newspaper, every theatre, every cinema and every advertisement hoarding must be brought into the service of this single mission until the panic-stricken prayer of our patriotic societies today: "Lord, set us free!" becomes, even in the brain of the smallest boy, the glowing plea: "Almighty God bless our arms on the day; be just as Thou ever wast. Judge now whether we merit freedom; Lord bless our fight!" All this has been neglected and nothing done.[2]

This is a book about propaganda, one more on a mounting pile of comments on a subject that has attracted scores of political scientists and sociologists over the past four decades. Its justification is that increasing interest in propaganda has led to greater concentration and specialization so that although there are today admirable new books on the processes of propaganda analysis or the factors that make some individuals more susceptible than others to the appeals of propaganda, and carefully prepared case-studies on the use of one special technique in one special set of circumstances, there are few up-to-date books that reduce this mass of specialized data to a systematic, coherent theory of propaganda. I have attempted here to provide such a synthesis, a book that, after surveying the field of literature on propaganda, presents in brief form a guide to the nature, mechanics, and ethics of social control through propaganda.

There have always been propagandists, some extremely skilled, but the continuing, institutionalized, large-scale attempt at mass political persuasion is a modern phenomenon, not fully developed before the First World War. The study of propaganda is even more recent for, apart from a few pioneering works at the turn of the present century, very little was written before 1930.

Any serious study of propaganda would seem to require, as a very minimum, agreement on the subject matter of that study. But to a large extent this has not yet been achieved. For the most part general treatises on propaganda have included purely nominal definitions drafted to support each author's particular line of argument. One of the tasks of this book, therefore, has been to consider the most important attempts to define the concept of propaganda, testing each first of all against the logical requirements of any good definition, and secondly against the actual activities of real propagandists. From this a new definition has been formulated, a definition which appears broad enough to embrace the full range of propaganda techniques and tactics and, at the same time, restrictive enough to distinguish propaganda from other related forms of activity.

Important to an understanding of propaganda is a knowledge of how and why it developed both as an activity and as an academic study. The answer is found in a peculiar combination of forces first appearing in nineteenth-century industrial society. The combined influence of Liberal and Rationalist philosophies, the extension of the franchise and the need to find methods of political persuasion to replace bribery and violence, the growth of population and its concentration in cities, a revolution in the technical means of communication commencing with the railways and culminating in radio and television, a rise in the general standard of living giving greater opportunities and incentives to take part in political activity, the spread of literacy, the beginnings of experimental psychology with its emphasis on the importance of unconscious and non-rational motivations, and the practical trial-and-error methods of commercial advertising, together produced a demand for large-scale persuasion, a technique of social control, the physical means of mass communication, and an audience equipped to absorb such appeals. Inevitably propaganda became a matter for the skilled professional rather than the inspired amateur.

But while politicians were beginning to use propaganda, and political scientists were beginning to study its machinery, there was little popular recognition of propaganda until the First World War. In addition to those special characteristics of nineteenth-century society which had led to the emergence of propaganda, the ideological character of the 1914-1918 war and the unprecedented nature of its operations played a further important part in stimulating greater interest in, and awareness of, propaganda. The effectiveness of Allied propaganda in hastening the collapse of German morale, or at least a general belief in its effectiveness, ensured that the propagandist would assist in the planning of every major military and political struggle from then on. The study of propaganda activities from 1914 to 1918 is also important in that it demonstrates the enormously wide range of activities regarded by propagandists as coming within the legitimate scope of their interest. Although most popular writing today regards propaganda essentially as a matter of lies and false claims, the men who were actually engaged in propaganda emphasized again and again that while they frequently sought to deceive both the enemy and the people on their own side, whenever possible they told the truth because the truth made more effective propaganda.

Once the war was over the flood of memoirs began. Then, as bit by bit the exploits of British, American, French and German propagandists became public knowledge, and as the Bolsheviks stepped up their campaign for international revolution, propaganda became a subject for intensive academic study. A difficulty arose from an unresolved confusion between propaganda meaning simply the propaganda of ideas, something undertaken by all belligerents, and propaganda meaning something basically dishonest which only the "enemy" did. Many who stated that they were considering propaganda in the first sense, demonstrated by their conclusions that they really thought of it in the second sense.

Propaganda is, of course, more than a definition. An understanding of the successes and failures of the propagandist requires also a knowledge of the techniques of propaganda, the machinery by which the propagandist conveys some idea to a larger audience. Propaganda, to be effective, must be seen, remembered, understood and acted upon. To achieve these aims it must be psychologically sound and adapted to the particular needs of the situation and the audience at which it is directed. Success also demands the selection of the most suitable means of communication, each of which has distinctive advantages and disadvantages. The study of propaganda thus extends into a study of communication media, of the relative strengths and weaknesses of press, film, radio and billboards, of the type of effect that might be achieved through the adoption of a distinguishing uniform, of the allies that might be gained, or lost, by writing a book or staging a parade complete with elephants and majorettes.

It is at this stage of tactical and strategical planning that propaganda evolves into psychological warfare, a form of combat exploited to the full by the Nazis and now the basis of the Cold War. Psychological warfare is the use of military, economic and political actions in conjunction with propaganda to demoralize the enemy, to discourage neutrals from joining him and to preserve morale at home. An enemy army will surrender only when it is no longer capable of effective resistance, but the number of lives that must be lost and the amount of material that must be destroyed before an army decides that further resistance is hopeless are relative values that can be affected by psychological warfare. Originally psychological warfare was designed as a preliminary to military action, demoralizing the enemy soldiers before the attack was launched, or as an aid to military action, hastening and cutting the cost of victory. Today it has become a substitute for military action. The Cold War is a bitterly fought contest in which each side makes a determined show of strength in order to discourage the other from attacking and while this goes on both sides strive to extend their influence by recruiting the uncommitted nations to their own cause. A defeat in the Cold War could be as real and as final as military defeat and, certainly, it would be followed by military defeat.

When the propaganda tactics of each side in the Cold War are compared, it is soon found that neither side has any inherent natural advantages. The different political systems mean that the East can adopt tactics simply not feasible in a democracy, but although this is true, it is also true that the West is free from the restraints of rigid dogmatism and undue centralism. But apart from these differences in approach the techniques of propaganda available to the modern dictator are not greatly different from those currently in use in the democracies. When one considers the total of all official and private sources of propaganda it can soon be seen that the volume of propaganda appeals in a democracy is almost certainly greater than in a dictatorship of comparable size. Yet, although he is not uniquely skilled in the arts of propaganda, the dictator appears able to mold the public mind to his will, to twist public opinion in any direction he wishes. The reason for this greater influence is, of course, the ability of the dictator to create a closed environment from which all ideas contrary to those of the official propagandist are excluded. The weapon of the dictator is not so much propaganda as censorship. The "propaganda menace" lies not in the volume or methods of propaganda but in a monopoly control over the means of communication to the exclusion of all propaganda hostile to the established order. Propaganda is a firmly established force in the political life of every modern state. Contrary to popular belief, it need not be a menace to the working of a system of representative democracy. For it is not propaganda that threatens the independence of the individual mind and creates a conditioned mass, but a monopoly control over the means of propaganda in the conditions of a closed society. It is the absence of the stimulus of conflicting ideas and of any alternative policies that result in the unquestioning uniformity of public opinion in the modern dictatorship. The protection of democracy therefore lies not in attempts to restrict or control the activities of propagandists but in providing the means for the propagation of all points of view.

Propaganda
and
Psychological Warfare

One

THE THEORY OF PROPAGANDA

In January, 1622, Pope Gregory XV reviewed the state of
the Church in Europe. Although religious wars had again
broken out in Bohemia, in Alsace, and in the Palatinate, the
Pope knew that it was now too late to reëstablish religious
unity by force of arms. New circumstances demanded new
measures to counteract the effects of the Protestant Refor-
mation. With all this in mind Pope Gregory announced his
intention to create a permanent, organized body for the
peaceful propagation of the Catholic faith. Subsequently,
on June 22 of that year, the *Sacra Congregatio Christiana
Nomini Propaganda* or, as it was more commonly known,
the *Sacra Congregatio de Propaganda Fide* became an official organ of the Roman Catholic Church with responsibility for carrying the faith to the new world, and for
strengthening and reviving it in the old. Although the *Sacra
Congregatio* was not the first official body to undertake
propaganda activities, it was the first to be so specifically
named.

Once the papal *Propaganda* was created, independent
action by individual churchmen gave way to a unified policy
directed and controlled from a central authority, which was
given, as part of its responsibility, a general supervision
over the content and format of liturgical books in use in
non-Catholic countries and the instruction of bishops and
other officials in the techniques of missionary activity.
Within a few years, in 1627, Pope Urban VIII founded the
Collegium Urbanum, the seminary of the *Propaganda,* providing a central training school for missionaries.

The work of the *Propaganda* was large-scale and "group-conscious," that is to say, it was directed, not at individuals as such, but at the "heathen masses of the Americas" and at the "protestant populations of Europe."

The methods and the detailed presentation of material were left to the discretion of those in the field, to be determined in the light of prevailing circumstances, subject only to the broad definitions of policy set down by the *Propaganda*. The object was to bring men to a voluntary acceptance of the Church's doctrines.[1]

Gregory's plan for the systematic propagation of Catholicism had two further effects not intended by its sponsor: it established a precedent later to be followed by others interested in the control of the opinions and, through them, the actions of men in the mass; and secondly, it suggested a convenient term for the modern practice of public opinion control. At first the word was used in its original sense, and applied to any organization set up to propagate a doctrine, but in time it was used to refer to the doctrine itself and finally to the techniques employed in spreading the doctrine. As might be expected with the example of the papacy before them, northern Protestant countries have given "propaganda" a sinister connotation which it does not have in southern Catholic lands. For an English writer in the nineteenth century it thus seemed quite logical to equate an organization for the spread of the Roman Catholic faith with any undesirable or subversive society. So we find in the 1840's an enthusiastic encyclopedist, W. T. Brande, concluding a brief historical outline of Gregory's organization with the comment:

> Derived from this celebrated society the name propaganda is applied in modern political language as a term of reproach to secret associations for the spread of opinions and principles which are viewed by most governments with horror and aversion.[2]

Apart from a few references such as that just quoted there was almost nothing written in English about propaganda from the seventeenth to the twentieth century. It then burst upon the world as one of the key words of the political scientist's vocabulary.

The activities of propaganda are, of course, not new, for the techniques of persuasion are as old as society. Since men first began to live in organized communities, the leaders, and those who aspired to leadership, have used the methods of propaganda to enlist a wider support. The pyramids of Egypt, the standards of the Roman legions, and the tribal totem poles of North America are propaganda in that they add to the mystique of leadership and, by consolidating the sense of "belonging," strengthen the unity and life of society. Atrocity stories designed either to shake the confidence of the enemy, or to arouse hatred against him, must be as old as war itself and every war has produced its record of the horrifying barbarities perpetrated by both sides.

Propaganda in the sense of a continuing, firmly established aspect of political life is, however, an essentially modern phenomenon because all the conditions for the emergence of large-scale, organized propaganda developed for the first time in the nineteenth-century national state and continue to exist today. These conditions, the prerequisites for mass propaganda, will be examined more fully in the next chapter.

At this stage it is enough to note that propaganda emerged slowly from the application of advertising techniques to politics to a highly specialized art in its own right. In the late nineteenth century a few far-seeing political scientists could envisage propaganda as a potential threat to democracy. By 1914, however, it had in fact replaced bribery and force as the principal means of enlisting the support of the many in the struggles of the politicians. But while political scientists wrote of it as a firmly entrenched aspect of contemporary politics, there were still comparatively few people who had even heard the word mentioned. The books of Wallas, Sorel, and Lippmann had reached only an intellectual minority, leaving the majority of men as yet unaware of the problem of propaganda.

The 1914-18 war, however, provided opportunities for experiments in practical propaganda on an unprecedented scale. By the end of the war a very large number of people had had first-hand experience of modern propaganda techniques. By the mid-1920's, when those who had taken part in these exercises began to publish their memoirs, the word itself had become popularized and incorporated into our regular political vocabulary.

The propaganda of the First World War, and especially that of the Allies in that war, will be examined later in some detail, first of all because it was the first systematic attempt to control public opinion over a fairly long period at both a national and an international level; and second because such a study involves a theoretical examination of the nature of propaganda. Many definitions of propaganda proposed in the 1930's are rejected here simply because they do not explain the activities of the self-professed propagandists of the war, and it is contended here that a theory of propaganda must, above all else, explain what propagandists do.

THE CONFUSION OF MEANINGS

By 1919, each of the great powers had built up a complex organization which established propaganda so firmly as a major weapon of power politics that political scientists could no longer justifiably disregard it in any analysis of political processes. But first they had to determine just exactly what they were studying, for there was now a great deal of confusion about the nature of propaganda. During the 1914-18 war, common usage had extended the meaning of the word far beyond its original reference without imposing any new universally recognized limits. It had been used both as a noun and as an adjective, as a form of abuse, as a synonym for the "lies" told by the other side, as a description of an activity as well as of the material used in that activity, and as a general term embracing aspects of what we now call psychological warfare. If political scientists were to succeed in systematizing their study, a re-definition of terms was clearly urgently required. Unfortunately their re-definition process proved more difficult than had been anticipated, and to a large extent it failed. It is part of the purpose of this chapter to review the various approaches to the question of definition.

A useful starting point is the definition put forward by R. J. R. G. Wreford in a paper published in 1923.[3] Wreford, after calling it a "hideous word" typical of an age renowned for its "etymological bastardy," suggested that propaganda be thought of as ". . . the dissemination of interested information and opinion." It was to be that and nothing more. The material disseminated could be either true or false, fact or opinion, for a good or for an evil cause. It was not essentially emotional in its appeal, nor was the method of dissemination relevant. All that was required was that it be "interested," that is to say that it originated in some group hoping to gain some advantage from the "sale" of a particular idea.

Wreford further defined "evil propaganda," which was distinct from ordinary propaganda, as propaganda that, while being interested, strove to appear disinterested. Evil propaganda disguised the propagandist's desire to influence opinion by pretending merely to inform. Although some later writers attempted to restrict the meaning of propaganda by confining it to those forms of persuasion in which the interest of the persuader was concealed, Wreford's argument that both open and concealed persuasion can be propaganda is much more reasonable and satisfactory.

Wreford's definition had brevity as a virtue, but brevity can be a weakness when too much is left unsaid. Propaganda is certainly the dissemination of interested opinion, but it is also more than that. From such a definition there is no means of telling whether its author would include in his concept of propaganda such things as the wearing of a uniform, the flying of a flag, or the whistling of a tune. On the face of it, Wreford's idea of propaganda was limited to the spread of ideas by the use of language whether spoken or written, and failed to provide for a wider range of propaganda activities. His definition also failed to recognize the purpose behind the dissemination of opinion, and it did not distinguish between opinions expressed by one individual to another in private argument and the dissemination of opinion by one individual to a whole nation. As the attempt at mass or group persuasion is the aspect of propaganda which concerns the political scientists, no study that ignores this factor can be regarded as truly adequate. But despite its inadequacies, Wreford's definition, by giving a lead to those who tried to eliminate the overtone of moral disapproval from propaganda per se, had a marked influence on the future development of propaganda studies.

Some years later, when H. D. Lasswell began to develop his scientific approach to politics, he formulated a definition which expressed ideas similar to Wreford's, although couched in very different terms. Propaganda, he wrote, "is the management of collective attitudes by the manipulation of the significant symbols." [4] Since this statement, apart from some minor variations in phrasing, is a basis for Lasswell's later writings, it is necessary to examine it in some detail. After defining propaganda, Lasswell began to explain his terms. An "attitude," he said, could be taken to mean a ". . . tendency to act according to certain patterns of valuation." [5] "Symbols" he had defined elsewhere as ". . . words, or word substitutes like pictures and gestures." [6] At this stage, Lasswell's idea of propaganda embraced the use of words, pictures, gestures, and so on, presented in such a way as to act on the political or other social standards of value of certain individuals with the intention of controlling the way those individuals will think and act. This concept, which comes very close to the heart of the matter of propaganda, became the basis of Lasswell's attempt to place propaganda and education in clearly separated and mutually exclusive departments, and it becomes therefore a suitable starting point for a more detailed discussion of the whole question of the relationship of these two phenomena.

Propaganda and Education

Propaganda and education are so obviously related in the general process by which opinions are formed that one is led immediately to compare them, but at the same time the

emotional connotations of the two words are so frankly
hostile that one feels obliged to separate them, to compare
them by stressing differences rather than by seeking similarities. Here the emotive overtones of the two words hin-
der our objective study of them. We *know* with such cer-
tainty that propaganda is absolutely opposed to education
that we must find some means of explaining away any common features. Like the efforts of the ancient astronomers
to explain the movements of the planets, the devices for
distinguishing propaganda from education have been many
and ingenious, but at best only partially successful.

Professor Lasswell has given a great deal of attention to
this question and his position has changed from time to
time. At one stage he put forward the argument that propaganda is concerned only with "controversial" attitudes,
while it was the duty of education to pass on "accepted"
attitudes and skills.[7] To illustrate this thesis Lasswell described how the teaching of Marxist economics in the Soviet
Union would be the teaching of an accepted attitude and
would therefore be education. In the United States, however, the teaching of such unaccepted and controversial
material as Marxist economics would be propaganda.

The obvious difficulty with this argument is its failure to
provide an agreed definition of the terms "acceptable" and
"controversial." Attitudes are often acceptable to those who
agree with them and controversial only to those who dispute
them. Although in the example quoted it is not too difficult
to determine the accepted and controversial attitudes, there
must be many people, even in the United States, who would
deny that there was anything in the least controversial
about Marxist economics. If all situations were no more
questionable than this, the classification could perhaps serve
some useful purpose, but this is obviously not so. It is possible to imagine many instances where it would be difficult
to decide between the accepted attitude, if any, and the controversial. At what stage, for example, in the conversion of
a country from capitalism to communism would Marxist
economics cease to be controversial and their teaching, in
consequence, become orthodox education instead of subver-

sive propaganda? A definition which leaves so much to subjective terms such as "acceptable" and "controversial" is of
little help in establishing an objective study.

It is difficult to understand why Lasswell departed from
the position he had taken in 1927. At that time, in *The
Theory of Political Propaganda* he contended that the word
"education" should be reserved to describe the "inculcation
of techniques," by which he meant the teaching of such
things as spelling, arithmetic, carpentry, and such like.
Propaganda, on the other hand, was "the creation of valu-
ational dispositions and attitudes," that is to say, the
forming of opinions about things.

As a standard for definition this position, if not entirely
adequate, was much more satisfactory than the one Lasswell later adopted. The value of the distinction made at
this stage was enhanced when, in the same paper, Lasswell
contrasted a "propagandist" attitude with a "deliberative"
attitude. A deliberative attitude, an essential feature of
education, implied that the quest for a solution would not
be prejudiced in favor of some particular solution selected
in advance. If the purpose of educational inquiry was truth,
the inquirers, if they were to remain true to the spirit of
education, could neither ignore nor suppress the truth, no
matter how unpopular it might be. A propagandist attitude,
in opposition to this, implied that the solution would be
determined before the search began. In other words, the
propagandist, with certain ends to achieve, looked to propaganda to bring out those objectives, to supply the evidence
to "prove" the solution he had already determined.

A distinction based on deliberative and propagandist attitudes is much more useful and realistic than one based on
acceptable and controversial attitudes, but there are still
some difficulties with Lasswell's definition. It is true, as
Lasswell suggested, that the propagandist it not normally
concerned with the inculcation of techniques. He does not
normally teach such things as spelling, arithmetic, or engineering, but this is only because these subjects do not
interest him in ordinary circumstances. The propagandist
may, on the other hand, find material in the way these sub-

jects are taught, in the fact that they are taught, or in the composition of the classes that learn them. Classroom material that is otherwise objective may also be used to carry propaganda on other themes, as for example, when the small child with his first arithmetic book is asked to add guns and soldiers rather than apples and oranges, or when the music class gives all its time to patriotic songs. The propaganda value of apparently non-political classroom material is seen in some Communist propaganda in which the theme of the regard of the Communist for the well-being of youth is illustrated by pictures of happy youngsters learning reading or carpentry or some other subject. The matter taught has itself little propaganda content, but its teaching is, nevertheless, part of a propaganda campaign. Again, it is not always easy to classify a textbook as propaganda or education simply by looking at it, for it may very well be both. Thus, a book on physics could be simply education for the physicist, but for the politician it might be valuable propaganda supporting his claim of the superiority of scientific research under his particular political system. By this type of classification, what is propaganda for one person could be education for another, and for the same person it could be education now and propaganda next year. It would be unwise, therefore, to dismiss the "inculcation of techniques" as something exclusive of and opposed to propaganda. Anything taught in the classroom may be propaganda if the propagandist so uses it, and in fact some of the world's most notorious propagandists have acknowledged the importance of the classroom in the dissemination of their ideas.

To appreciate the approach of another American, L. W. Doob, to this question of education and propaganda, it is first of all necessary to examine his theories of "suggestion." This in turn requires that one begin with Doob's understanding of the word "attitude." The significance of this term is discussed at length in *Propaganda, Its Psychology and Technique*,[8] but this lengthy and sometimes complicated treatment neither materially expands nor restricts the meaning of "attitude" from its generally accepted use as that broad, and necessarily imprecise, combination of psychological factors within a person that in part determine how that person shall react to any given situation.

After defining a "stimulus-situation" as anything which aroused an attitude,[9] Doob came to his definition of "suggestion":

> Suggestion results from the manipulation of stimulus-situation in such a way that, through the consequent arousal of pre-existing, related attitudes there occurs within the mental field a new integration which would not have occurred under different stimulus-situations.[10]

The key words in this definition were "manipulation" and "arousal of pre-existing, related attitudes."

The idea of suggestion therefore implied that there were within the individual certain existing attitudes to any particular problem. These attitudes were neither fixed nor immutable, but could be affected by external influences called "stimulus-situations." Any event, any incident, speech, picture or book, any person or object which caused some reaction in the observer, could be a stimulus-situation. Certain stimulus-situations could be controlled or manipulated by other individuals and when pre-existing attitudes were changed to the extent of creating new attitudes through such controlled stimulus-situations the operation was called "suggestion."

Non-suggestion occurred when there was mere perception of the stimulus-situation without any consequent impact on attitudes, or when any changes in an individual's attitudes as a result of that perception were not dependent upon the arousal of pre-existing attitudes.

This theory can best be understood through an example. Consider, first of all, a man frustrated and jealous of those more prosperous than himself (these are the pre-existing attitudes) who receives a pamphlet (the stimulus-situation) to the effect that he is kept in poverty by the machinations of Jewish financiers. This stimulus-situation, acting on his pre-existing attitudes, has the effect of arousing in him a new feeling of anti-Semitism (the new attitude) and the process can therefore be called suggestion.

On the other hand, should the same pamphlet be received by an economist with his own well-informed views on the role of Jewish and other financiers and be read by him without there being any change in his attitudes, then there is mere perception and, therefore, non-suggestion.

Doob further distinguished between direct and indirect suggestion. In direct suggestion in which the individual sees, as part of the stimulus-situation, the suggester's immediate aim, there are aroused in him auxiliary and related attitudes to the suggester as well as to his suggestion. If the suggestion is successful then the new attitudes would include comprehension of the suggester's aim and they might, or might not, lead to the action desired by the suggester. An example of direct suggestion is the advertisement where the reader is fully aware that the sole purpose of the skillful photography and enthusiastic prose is to sell him a car. Because he is aware that the advertisement is a piece of special pleading by a named advertiser he is more likely to be able to make an individual decision about it. His acceptance of the message is, in part, governed by his existing attitude to the advertiser. In indirect suggestion the suggester's purpose is concealed. He does not specifically recommend his product, but builds up a favorable reaction to it by other means; for example, an apparently genuine and unsolicited statement from a medical research team that tobacco treated with chemical "x" will not cause lung cancer. This would be indirect suggestion if no reference was made to the fact that the research team was employed or sponsored by the makers of a brand of cigarettes treated with "x." Doob argued that because the identity and purpose of the suggester are concealed, indirect suggestion is more dangerous to society, but is likely to be more successful than direct suggestion in bringing about the results desired by the suggester.

At this stage Doob began to develop a thesis which led him away from the general current of thought on propaganda. He insisted that the key to propaganda lay in the

attempt to "control attitudes . . . through the use of suggestion." [11] It was not essential that the use of suggestion
should be intended, or even that it should be understood:

> If individuals are controlled through the use of sugges-
> tion . . . then the process may be called propaganda,
> regardless of whether or not the propagandist intends to
> exercise the control. On the other hand if individuals are
> affected in such a way that the same result would be
> obtained with or without the aid of suggestion, then this
> process may be called education, regardless of the intention
> of the educator.[12]

This is the essence of Doob's theory of unintentional propaganda which, by reducing propaganda to a psychological
phenomenon, divorced it from any ethical or emotive connotations. As such, it was a considerable advance in objective thinking on the subject, although there were still a
number of objections and difficulties.

Certainly a great deal of propaganda is circulated by persons who do not fully understand the process of "suggestion" and who would have no intention of consciously disseminating propaganda. During the Hitler regime, for example there must have been many German schoolteachers
who unconsciously and in all good faith indoctrinated their
pupils with the propaganda of militaristic nationalism. But
it is a mistake to assume that there was any unintentional
propaganda here. All the Nazi propaganda was the deliberate creation of those interested in fostering a warlike
patriotic nationalism, although most of it reached its
audience through the unwitting assistance of others. The
schoolteachers were not unintentional propagandists; they
were educators who were also the unintentional instruments
for the distribution of the intentional propaganda of their
political leaders. All propaganda is intentional, even that
which is disseminated by people not fully aware of the
significance of their actions.

In opposition to Doob, the thesis is put forward here
that the very essence of the distinction between propaganda
and education is the deliberate nature of propaganda. Anything that is taught to anyone, anywhere, is propaganda if

—but only if—it is deliberately disseminated by someone conscious of its propaganda function. To use Doob's terminology, suggestion can be propaganda, but only if the manipulation of stimulus-situations is understood and intended.

The purpose of propaganda is to control actions by influencing attitudes. The propagandist does not distribute his material because he wants others to share some newly-discovered truth any more than he lies out of some malicious pleasure in deceiving, but he does both because he hopes that his message will encourage those who hear it to do as he wants them to do. In contrast to education, where the matter taught is fixed within the limits of currently available knowledge, the material and techniques of propaganda are variables to be selected according to their supposed efficacy in getting results.

In short, the existence of propaganda has nothing to do with either the objective truth of the material taught or the belief in its truth, but is entirely dependent upon the intention of the propagandist to use the material taught to affect in some desired manner the attitudes of his audience toward specific situations. The relationship between what is taught and the attitudes it is designed to affect may be obvious or obscure.

To return to Doob: For him, suggestion occurred whenever a stimulus-situation was manipulated in such a way that "through the consequent arousal of pre-existing, related attitudes" there arose a new attitude. In contrast to this, non-suggestion was the result of a mere perception of the stimulus-situation without any change in pre-existing attitudes. Thus, as Doob himself admitted, what was suggestion, and consequently propaganda, for one man would not always be propaganda for another. The example of the anti-Semitic pamphlet used earlier in this chapter illustrates this point quite well. Such a notion makes any scientific study of the extent or even the existence of propaganda quite impossible, for it would demand that the observer should examine the altered attitudes, if any, of every person who perceived that propaganda. This is one of the most serious objections to Doob's whole argument. The criterion for determining the existence of propaganda is "suggestion," the basis of "suggestion" is the "arousing of pre-existing attitudes," but there is no process for discovering the presence of such pre-existing attitudes nor for measuring the extent to which they have been modified, except perhaps by clinical examination of particular individuals. By Doob's theory there is no justification in describing Einstein's Relativity Theory as education, nor in calling Hitler's speeches propaganda; it all depends on the individual who perceives these things. Doob's definition of propaganda was finally dependent upon the receptive ability of each individual. Propaganda became an effect, rather than a process.

In his later writings Doob abandoned the idea of suggestion as a distinction between propaganda and education because it was, in his view, psychologically inadequate.[13] It had failed, he said, to recognize the existence of social customs and conventions which could be learned with or without suggestion but which were clearly not part of the strict education process. Unfortunately Doob's alternative was even less successful than his idea of suggestion for he now sought to recognize propaganda by an ethical evaluation of the material disseminated. Education was ". . . the imparting of knowledge or skill considered to be scientific or to have a survival value in a society at a particular time," [14] while propaganda was ". . . the attempt to affect the personalities and to control the behaviour of individuals towards ends considered unscientific or of doubtful value in a society at a particular time." [15]

The main objection to this classification is that it does not explain all the activities commonly accepted as propaganda. It is not unreasonable to argue that if a generally recognized and self-admitted propagandist uses material acknowledged to be scientifically objective for purposes which he, the propagandist, asserts to be propaganda, then it must be agreed that the dissemination of scientifically objective material can be propaganda. That such material has been used by propagandists is one of the more obvious facts which emerge from a study of propaganda in the First World War, and an examination of propaganda techniques in common use today simply confirms this argument. The United States government, for example, has realized the value of exploiting for propaganda purposes American technical and industrial superiority. As part of its Cold War campaign, designed to enhance the prestige of the United States against the Soviet Union, it has encouraged and sponsored such things as advertising by American firms in the foreign press, the release of American patents to underdeveloped countries, and the exchange of experts in various fields of education and technology.[16] These things are, in part, propaganda, because propagandists are using them as such, but the release of a patent is "the imparting of knowledge considered to be scientific" and is therefore, by Doob's definition, education.

Doob himself recognized some of the difficulties of his definition although apparently he did not realize the extent to which these difficulties invalidated his whole argument. He acknowledged, for example, that anyone attempting to distinguish education and propaganda would have to be "aware of the state of scientific knowledge on a subject" and he would have to be "conscious of the value judgements" he used in his own thinking. When one discovers the heat and passion with which geneticists debated Lysenko's theories, or physicists philosophize on indeterminism in quantum theory, it is easy to conclude that, if in even these unemotive and supposedly demonstrable sciences there is no universal agreement on the true state of scientific knowledge, the probability of there being any unanimity on the exact limits of scientific knowledge in politics or economics is so remote that it can be discounted. Doob has defined propaganda by terms which are themselves indefinable and his definition is therefore unsatisfactory.

Many other definitions of propaganda and education have been formulated for the purpose of distinguishing these two phenomena. While few of these originated in the systematic arguments of political scientists and therefore generally lack any logical validity, they demand some comment for they are the product of the broad social and political thinking of our society.[17]

Some popular views, such as the idea that "education deals with the instruction of childhood; propaganda consists in efforts to affect adult behavior," [18] or that "education consists in the things which are taught in schools, propaganda in things taught outside schools," [19] are so obviously inadequate that they do not require further refutation, but others do require more detailed examination.

Because of the widespread political practice of using the word "propaganda" as a pejorative term for exposing the "falsehoods" of one's opponents, the association of propaganda and lying has become deeply ingrained in the popular mind. Yet it is an association that will not stand up under objective criticism. Experience of wartime propaganda makes it quite clear that a great deal of undoubted propaganda, including some of the so-called falsehoods of our opponents, really consists of undeniable fact. On the other hand it is also necessary to recognize that not everything usually accepted as education can be labeled incontrovertible fact. In all discussion and teaching of the social sciences, especially history, economics and political science, there is inevitably a personal interpretation of facts which are regarded as significant. Practical experience has demonstrated the impossibility of excluding subjective evaluations or opinions from lectures on, say, the British welfare state or the American Supreme Court. Much of the teaching of history consists of explaining and evaluating facts, themselves disputed, and assigning causes and consequences to events which may or may not have happened as recorded. "Fact" and "fiction" are terms too tenuous to serve as terms of reference in a definition. Even the examples and problems one uses in algebra and arithmetic often embody some implied judgments of economic institutions.

Another basis of classification is to make the criterion the purpose of the teaching rather than the matter taught, a distinction which may be expressed by defining education as being "motivated by service to society as a whole" while propaganda "is devoted to advancing the interest of a special group." [20] This interpretation requires one to distinguish among rival propagandists all acting in the belief that they are public benefactors seeking to put the good of society above that of a sectional group. But the "good of society" is not an objective term, a standard by which other acts may be impartially judged. Ever since Locke and Rousseau, men have been forced to recognize that the good of society is in practice indistinguishable from the good of the numerical majority or from the good of a vociferous minority which has been able to get itself accepted as a majority. A classification based on the good of society usually means simply that the advocating of things "our side" wants is education, while the dissemination of the views of the "other side" is propaganda. Even the most well-intentioned people find it difficult to recognize a concern for the good of society in the claims of groups that they oppose. This kind of definition leads to the final absurdity that all propagandists are on the other side.

A final case to be examined is the thesis that education transmits the social inheritance while propaganda indoctrinates people with a desire to alter the social system. As with the definition based on the good of society, the difficulty here is the question of delimitation. Since there is no fixed, static set of facts and theories that constitute *the* social inheritance someone must decide what elements make up our social inheritance and which parts of this should be passed on to future generations. It would be extremely naïve to expect any wide agreement on such a matter. So long as our society does not become stagnant, every program for its development must owe something to the past and therefore must be in some way part of the social heritage. Both Communist and Capitalist today can validly claim to be passing on the social inheritance of the Liberal-industrial revolution, as can the white colonists in Rhodesia and the African nationalists in Nigeria. It is not even possible to distinguish those groups that wish to preserve unchanged some aspect of our inheritance from those who would alter it, for in even the most conservative of communities the status quo is more a slogan than a fact of life. It is not a question of change *versus* stability, but a matter of the direction of change.

The "good of society" and the "transmission of the social inheritance" are fine sounding phrases. They accord with our ideals of what should be the objectives of the good and just society. They are things we want. But as a basis for definition they are valueless, for when they are applied to specific situations they become nothing more than the dignified robes by which men disguise their deeply ingrained prejudices.

From the study of these various theories, and others of lesser importance, certain conclusions about the relationship between education and propaganda can now be postulated. Despite the widespread belief that it should be so, the two phenomena are clearly not mutually exclusive. Although certain forms of promotion belong solely to one or the other, certain further activities can be included justly in either field.

Thus the propagandist is not normally concerned with one of education's major activities, the teaching of skills, or what Lasswell called the "inculcation of techniques," although, as has already been pointed out, it is unwise to make too rigid a division, for the propagandist can find material in almost any aspect of an education program. On the other hand, the deliberate dissemination of what is known to be false in order to arouse favorable attitudes is a form of propaganda quite hostile to the spirit of education, which teaches what is believed to be true in the light of currently available knowledge. The criterion of education is not so much "truth" in some absolute objective sense, as it is a sincere belief in the truth of some particular opinion. Then again, such instances of propaganda as parades, uniforms, postage stamps, martial music, and so on, are only indirectly related to education even though they may contribute in various ways to school life.

But between these extremes there is a wide range of activities that belong in both fields. Propaganda is the attempt to influence opinions; much education, especially in the social sciences, deals as much with opinions about facts as with facts themselves. The very nature of these subjects demands the expression of value judgments and usually means that those who have informed opinions spend much of their time trying to convince others of the correctness of their interpretation. Such expressions of opinion, if delivered in good faith by persons believing in their objective truth and worth, are education, but in so far as there is also the intention that those hearing them should develop certain specific attitudes towards them, they are also propaganda. This intention must be present, at least in some slight degree, in the minds of most of those engaged in teaching politics and economics, but this does not mean that their efforts are not genuinely educational.

The argument can be summarized in a few sentences. If the material taught is known to be untrue, but is taught as truth with the conscious intent to deceive, it can be propaganda, but not education. If, on the other hand, it is honestly believed to be truth, and is taught as such, it can be either propaganda or education or both. Irrespective of whether it is true or not, if it is intended to influence attitudes in specific directions it is propaganda. In short, most of the attempts to distinguish propaganda and education have failed because they have not recognized that the criteria of the two phenomena are quite different. The standard of education is the truth of the material in the light of available knowledge. The standard of propaganda is the purpose behind the teaching. Where the purpose is achieved by the teaching of what is believed to be the truth then the result is both propaganda and education.

Truth and Rationality

The popular association of propaganda with false or irrational forms of persuasion has its origin, first of all, in the common political practice of contrasting "our" publicity and information services with "their" propaganda trickery, and persists even when closer examination reveals more similarities than contrasts. It stems secondly from the moral and intellectual indignation of those who were shocked by the revelations after the First World War of the extent to which even "our" side spread lies to play on the irrational motivations of both friend and foe.

Even so eminent a scholar as James Bryce could, in 1921, accept uncritically the then popular attack on the war propagandists, and he defined propaganda as "that dissemination by the printed word of untruths and fallacies and incitements to violence." [21] Propaganda, as Bryce understood it, was essentially immoral, gathering its strength from the weaknesses of public opinion. It had become a highly specialized art wherein skilled practitioners could, by false and one-sided statements, "beguile and mislead" those unable or unwilling to find the facts for themselves.

Although the linking of propaganda with falsehood first became widespread in the years after 1918, a more careful examination of the exploits of the wartime propagandists will demonstrate the insubstantial foundation of this association. The accounts of war propaganda in Chapter Three will lead one inevitably to the conclusion that all propaganda cannot justifiably be identified with lies. Certainly propagandists lied, by suppression at least, more often than they told the truth, and possibly the total effect of their combined efforts was deception; nevertheless, they made an impartial presentation of facts often enough to prove that they also told the truth. Their propaganda was not, in principle, devoted to either truth or falsehood, but to persuasiveness. The propagandists were prepared to use either facts or lies, depending on which were thought to be most effective in convincing an audience. Any theory of propaganda which ignores this point by trying to correlate propaganda with falsehood must therefore be rejected as insufficient.

The most effective way of countering a too-easy linking of propaganda with false and irrational appeal is thus by reference to the activities of actual propagandists. But apart from this appeal to facts, there are other considerations of a more theoretical nature that can be dealt with here.

There is, first of all, the difficulty of deciding just what is a lie, for it is obvious that not all untrue statements are lies. There are three essential elements to a lie: the material must be untrue; it must be known to be untrue; and it must be told with the intention to deceive. But while these things are necessary to constitute a lie, they can be extremely difficult to recognize in practice. There are many situations where one could not fairly distinguish between a conscious misrepresentation of fact and an innocent mistake.

The consequences of this type of confusion have been well brought out by the reporting of the air battles in the Second World War. During the Battle of Britain, from July to October 1940, the British radio and press services gave details of the heavy losses of German aircraft, officially accepted as accurate by the British air defense authorities, although they were subsequently proved to have been greatly exaggerated. The inaccuracies arose largely from the faulty reporting of those who claimed to have destroyed the enemy planes. Two or three fighter pilots might each claim the same enemy bomber; Fighter Command might shoot down a plane damaged and reported as destroyed by anti-aircraft guns; a plane reported as shot down at sea might actually limp back to France and be repaired. The total effect of all these false claims was staggering. In the month of September 1940 alone, the British claimed to have destroyed 1,108 enemy aircraft although later checking of German records showed the number to have been only 582. For the whole four-months' period of the Battle of Britain the number of victories claimed was 2,698; the actual number of German aircraft destroyed was 1,733.[22]

We would scarcely be justified in calling those responsible for issuing the original figures liars because they were, for the most part, acting in good faith and presenting what they believed to be true. On the other hand, when the British bombing of Germany increased in intensity and the Germans began, for similar reasons, to make similar exaggerated claims of British losses, the British asserted that these false claims proved the Germans were liars. The attitude generally is that when "we" tell an untruth it is a mistake made in good faith, but when "they" make the same mistake it is a lie.

A further problem arises from the fact that the recognition of the lie, and therefore of the propaganda, depends on the knowledge of those who receive the message. There must be many situations where false statements, including some deliberate lies, pass unchallenged and therefore unidentified as propaganda because the one who received the message was even less informed than the one who delivered it.

Apart from the fact that any survey of the activities of propagandists, whether in wartime or in peacetime domestic politics, establishes beyond all doubt that most of them do tell the truth at least some of the time, the problems discussed above demonstrate that the practical difficulties of applying such terms as "truth" and "irrationality" make these terms valueless as a means of identifying propaganda.

Concealed Propaganda

One of the best known writers on propaganda, F. E. Lumley, approached his study with the conviction that propaganda was a menace, and he tended to find value only in those arguments which supported this conviction. Nevertheless, despite his subjective attitude, Lumley merits attention for he has presented in their most consistent form some of the more popular ideas about propaganda.

Lumley was one of a small group of pioneers who in the 1920's began to examine the wider implications of the propaganda experiences of the First World War and to attempt to explain propaganda in sociological-psychological terms. His first definition appeared in 1929 [23] and at this stage he concluded that propaganda was nothing more nor less than "the dissemination of conclusions"—a definition that has much to commend it but which really refers only to one form of propaganda.

A few years later, in *The Propaganda Menace*,[24] when he again began inquiring into the nature of propaganda, he

apparently realized the inadequacy of a definition confined
to one distinguishing characteristic when there are other
characteristics just as essential to an understanding of the
concept. His second definition was expressed in terms which
went far beyond his original pithy comment:

> Propaganda is promotion which is veiled in one way or
> another as to (1) its origins or sources; (2) the interests
> involved; (3) the methods employed; (4) the content
> spread; and (5) the results accruing to the victims:—any
> one, any two, any three, any four, or all five.[25]

By this definition and the evidence he provided to sub-
stantiate it, Lumley fell into a logical trap. He formulated
a hypothesis (that propaganda was a sinister influence)
from which he deduced certain characteristics (the veiled
features just listed), which were in turn used to prove the
matter-of-fact validity of the original hypothesis.

It was not difficult for Lumley to find instances of propaganda where the propagandist's identity was concealed.
But before the fact of concealed origin could be asserted
as fundamental to the nature of propaganda it would be
necessary to argue that wherever one finds some example
of promotion in which the identity of the promoter is hid-
den, then there is propaganda. This would demand that we
treat proverbs, much anonymous poetry, the great majority
of folk songs, and many of the best-known hymns as propaganda, however and whenever they are used, for they are
all forms of promotion where the origin is veiled. Such a
notion is so far from any accepted reference of the term
propaganda that it can be discarded.

The other four points of concealment mentioned by
Lumley can be rejected for the same reasons. Each, if applied without qualification, makes an unreasonable and
often absurd extension of what is commonly understood
by propaganda.

Some confusion has probably stemmed from uncertainty
as to what exactly Lumley meant by "veiled." If he intended to imply that the origin could not be discovered,
then propaganda would have to be restricted to a very few
of its most skillfully concealed forms: probably only those

examples so artfully disguised that their apparent origin would never be questioned and consequently their existence as propaganda never suspected.

What was more probably at the back of Lumley's mind was that if the propagandist consciously tried to hide his identity then there was propaganda, even though at some later stage his identity might be revealed. But even this leads to difficulty. For example, is a cartoonist who signs his work with a pseudonym as does, say, Vicky in the London *Daily Mirror,* a propagandist? Or is the identification of his work with a particular newspaper enough to claim that the origin is not veiled at all? And could the work of so widely known a cartoonist as Herblock of the *Washington Post* ever be considered veiled, even if reproduced without acknowledgment to the *Washington Post?* It is obviously not enough to be able to say "I do not know where this comes from, therefore it is propaganda." The observer must find some test for distinguishing promotion whose origin has been deliberately concealed from promotion where the origin is just simply not known at a particular time to a particular person.

The same criticism can be made of the other "veiled" characteristics in Lumley's definition. In each instance there is room for considerable disagreement on whether the thing is veiled or not. The propagandist, for example, is not necessarily hiding the interests behind his efforts if he fails to make specific reference to these in every instance. He may assume, with justification, that his association with certain interests is so well known that it does not have to be mentioned. Yet there may still be many who are not aware of his associations and who therefore would charge him, in perfectly good faith, of hiding the interests which support him.

A NEW DEFINITION

It is now possible to put forward a new definition of propaganda which may be of some value in assessing the use which is made or which should be made of propaganda in international society. The guiding principle in drafting this definition is that it be sufficient to cover every activity of those generally recognized as propagandists, to see what is common to this activity, and to exclude all else. Propaganda is thus defined as the deliberate attempt by some individual or group to form, control, or alter the attitudes of other groups by the use of the instruments of communication, with the intention that in any given situation the reaction of those so influenced will be that desired by the propagandist. The propagandist is the individual or group who makes any such attempt.

In the phrase, "the deliberate attempt," lies the key to the idea of propaganda. This is the one thing that marks propaganda from non-propaganda. In the preceding pages it has been established beyond doubt that anything may be used as propaganda and that nothing belongs exclusively to propaganda. It seems clear, therefore, that any act of promotion can be propaganda only if and when it becomes part of a deliberate campaign to induce action through the control of attitudes. Let it be once established that any statement, any book, poster, or rumor, any parade or exhibition, any statue or historic monument, any scientific achievement, any abstract of statistics, whether true or false, rational or irrational in appeal or presentation, originates as the deliberate policy of someone trying to control or alter attitudes, then that thing may be regarded as part of the instruments or material of propaganda. An investigator wishing to study the volume or nature of the propaganda of any society or age must first prove the existence of the propaganda by tracing each instance of promotion that he proposes to examine back to a propagandist. This may often be difficult to do, but until the given example of suspected propaganda is positively identified as part of a deliberate and conscious policy for the control of group attitudes, it cannot be classified as propaganda.

Propaganda is, secondly, the attempt to "form, control or alter the attitudes of other groups." It is a basic assumption of all attempts at public-opinion control that "attitudes," which in part determine how each individual will react to specific situations, are affected by outside influences which are in turn partly controllable. The propagandist consciously tries to control those external influences, sometimes to create an attitude to a new situation, sometimes to strengthen attitudes which already exist and preserve them against disruptive forces, and sometimes to change undesirable attitudes to others more favorable to his own cause.

A third point is that propaganda is addressed to the group, rather than to single individuals as such. This large-scale aspect of the propagandist's activities is, however, more a question of convention than of the intrinsic nature of propaganda. That is to say, there need not be any essential difference between the efforts of one individual to persuade another and the efforts of the same individual to persuade a whole class, but the term propaganda is customarily reserved for the latter case alone. Propaganda has a social significance; it interests political scientists and sociologists because it is an attempt to control such large groups as "the youth of the nation," the "floating vote," the "working class," or the "nation" itself. There is no precise point in size, no exact numerical minimum for the audience which determines when a form of promotion shall be called propaganda. Because propaganda is primarily the effort of a few to appeal to large groups it is a form of promotion that interests men to the extent of giving it a special name and making it an object of special study. Any particular example of promotion which is on a scale large enough to attract the serious attention of at least one observer therefore can validly be treated as propaganda.

The definition refers to the attempt to control attitudes "by the use of the instruments of communication." This phrase, "the instruments of communication," which will be dealt with more fully in Chapter Four, is an omnibus word to cover any and all means of communicating an idea from man to man. It is generally what Lasswell had in mind when he talked of "symbols." It embraces language whether spoken or written and however expressed, all forms of graphic representation, music, displays and exhibitions, and generally almost anything that can be perceived by eye or ear. Although this great catholicity in the selection and availability of the instruments of communication invalidates any attempt to make a primary identification of propaganda through its instruments, the fact that such communication is used does distinguish propaganda from persuasion by bribery or the use of violence. The propagandist may promise riches or threaten violence, or he may point to riches amassed and the violence suffered by others, but he does not, as a propagandist, actually bribe or inflict that violence. The propagandist does not compel others to do his bidding; he is content to create the conditions under which others will apparently wish to do what he wants.

An important feature of propaganda is indicated by the words "with the intention that in any given situation the reaction of those influenced will be that desired by the propagandist." The propagandist can thus be seen as one who, having envisaged some existing or possible future situation, tries to create in others some specific attitude to that situation, which will in turn lead to some desired action. The propagandist is after results. He hopes that those listening to his message will eventually do something he wants them to do. The matter disseminated and the form of its dissemination are variables to be selected according to their supposed efficacy in bringing about the desired result. The goal of the propagandist is not just a change in attitudes, but a change in attitudes that results in action. This means, for example, that a propagandist for a new party in an established two-party system must not only convince the electorate of the wisdom of his party's policies, but he must also persuade them that a vote for a third party is not a wasted vote. The vote is the measure of his success, not the change in opinion.

The identification of the propagandist in the terms of the definition just stated is not a matter of personal discretion or subjective valuation. The propagandist is one seeking to control the attitudes of other groups for certain specific purposes. No consideration of the moral or political nature of those ends or of the means he adopts is relevant.

Under the terms of this definition, the potential propagandists are all groups calling themselves propaganda agencies, all Ministries of National Enlightenment, Psychological Warfare Departments, Departments of National Morale,
all Offices of War Information, the Propaganda, Information or Public Relations Departments of all political parties,
governments and politically directed groups, the editors
and publishers of all newspapers advocating a particular
political policy, whether as a consistent practice or as an
isolated piece of special pleading, all politicians in their
official capacities, the spokesmen of all such groups as
Trade Unions, Employers' Associations, Temperance Societies, National Liberation Committees, and all other
groups advocating or opposing some specified political,
economic, or social policy. One is entitled to assume that
when these people or groups speak, they do so deliberately,
and that their attempt to influence our attitudes is part of
a conscious policy. Other groups, such as Education Departments and individual authors and speakers, would be
propagandists if they worked deliberately for some particular ideology. Again we are entitled to assume that, if an
author writes a book attacking socialism, he intended to
do so and we can therefore call him a propagandist.

Therefore, the first problem of the political scientist setting out to analyze some particular manifestation of suspected propaganda is to prove that the material he has in
mind originates as part of the deliberate policy of a propagandist. Although obtaining proof may sometimes be difficult, especially when one is considering such esoteric matters as the political symbolism of architectural styles, it is
the necessary first step to the identification of propaganda
significance. He must prove that the thing he is examining
was intended to have this significance. Fortunately, the
question of origin is one of fact and should not be in any
way influenced by the observer's ethical valuations, and it
would normally be enough to find that something originated
with an accepted propagandist organization to classify it as
propaganda.

Let us now evaluate the complete definition of propaganda proposed here according to the standard requirements of any definition. First, it appears to fulfill the function for which it was intended, for by removing the identification of propaganda from the field of personal evaluation or knowledge or, at least, by reducing the significance of subjective evaluations, it should encourage a scientific analysis. It would enable men of different political opinions to feel confident that they are talking about the same thing. Second, there is an identity of concepts. The definition is extensive enough to embrace every possible example of propaganda; yet it effectively excludes everything else. Third, the defining characteristics are themselves reasonably capable of objective investigation. Ambiguous or emotional words such as "honest," "irrational," "biased," or "one-sided" are minimized. In this way the identity of the propagandist can become a question of observable fact because no account need be taken of his moral, social or political motives; if his objective is to influence public attitudes, then he is a propagandist. Finally, the definition fits the observable features of propaganda activity. It explains exactly the purpose and policy of such organization as Goebbel's Ministry for People's Enlightenment and Propaganda, or the British "Crewe House" in the First World War. It includes everything which people generally accept as propaganda, so that, although it clarifies the common usage of the word, it does not distort such usage.

On the basis of this definition an ordinarily competent investigator could begin a survey of the extent or nature of the propaganda within a given society and could expect that other investigators with different standards of ethics or politics would, given the same information, reach generally similar conclusions.

Two

THE DEVELOPMENT OF
PROPAGANDA

AN AUDIENCE FOR THE PROPAGANDIST

Modern mass propaganda came into existence as a major
political force because of the emergence in the nineteenth-
century industrial state of a peculiar combination of
circumstances. These circumstances, reinforced by other
aspects of twentieth-century life, continue to influence the
way our political affairs are conducted. Thus, before
propaganda could assume its present importance, it was
first of all necessary that the politically ambitious members
of the community should need to gain the apparently willing allegiance of the uninterested majority. This is a state
of affairs which arises only when the political leaders are
at least formally dependent for their authority upon the
support of the ruled. In other societies the masses could
be ignored or, in crisis, quelled by violence or fear. But
with the gradual acceptance of a belief in universal suffrage,
of the concept of subjects as wise as their masters, there
came the idea that the rulers should seek the verdict of
public opinion, not reluctantly when circumstances made
it inevitable, but at all times as something which was in
itself right and proper. Politicians came to learn that their
right to rule was meaningless without its periodic acceptance
by the normally politically uninterested people. This awareness of the commanding authority of popular approval
became, in part, the inspiration of the *Federalist* essays at
the end of the eighteenth century. The power-conscious

members of the community saw in the techniques of propaganda a way to obtain popular backing that, in the changed circumstances of the day, would be more effective than bribery or force.

Even those whose attitude toward the role of public opinion in politics did not change found that of necessity they had to learn the mechanics of peaceful persuasion by propaganda. With an extended franchise and an increasing population it was becoming too expensive to do anything else. Where at one time voters could be bought, they had now to be persuaded. Politicians had, therefore, good reason to become interested in propaganda.

Implicit in the word propaganda today is the idea of large-scale promotion of ideas. Sociologists and political scientists study propaganda because with it individuals and small groups attempt to control the thoughts and actions, not of individuals as such, but of economic classes, religions, races, political parties or nations. This notion of "mass" persuasion, although it is extremely useful, is, however, vague and ill-defined. It is quite impossible to set a precise limit on the size of the audience needed in order to classify actions as propaganda or non-propaganda. All that can be said is that if the activity is extensive enough to attract the serious attention of sociologists or political scientists, then it is broad enough to be thought of as possible propaganda requiring further examination. It is because propaganda usually is an attempt at large-scale formation of opinion that it has become politically significant.

Although the propagandist is interested primarily in large-scale persuasion, it should not be concluded from this that he must always speak directly to the people at large. There are many situations where the propagandist's purposes are achieved more effectively through influencing the opinions of leaders, whether of organized groups or of a broader society. Thus, whereas the propagandist of one group might try to appeal directly to the public, another might hold a dinner and reception for the local newspaper editors. Much wartime and Cold War propaganda is directed at highly specialized audiences—industrialists, professors, scientists, and so on. Many interested groups by their very nature have extremely limited popular appeal and exert such influence as they have on a minority of intellectual, wealthy, or politically important people. Yet most of this appeal still fits into the context of mass propaganda, for the general intention is, in most cases, to influence the many by influencing the few who lead society.

However imprecise the concept of "mass audience" may be, it nevertheless has meaning and is important to an understanding of the origins of propaganda, for the propagandist's audience is made up of large differentiated groups susceptible to a "group-directed" approach. There must be, therefore, not only groups, but groups aware of their separate identity as such and possessing a feeling · of "group-consciousness," that sense of unity within the group by which the individuals recognize their group membership and are able to understand and to respond to appeals to their common interest. An awareness of one's status or role is important for the success of propaganda. Although the propagandist speaks directly to the group, he fails unless he makes some impact on the individual members of the group and he will so fail when the individuals are insufficiently conscious of their group identity.

The rapid growth and concentration of population which followed industrialization in nineteenth-century Europe provided the setting for such an emergent group-consciousness. Throughout that period there was a steady shift of population from the country to the new cities where both the increasing size of factories and the concentration of their workers in overcrowded houses made men more than ever aware of their social and economic class. A man working with, say, nine others in a village factory could well feel a loyalty to his employer stronger than any sense of common interest with other workers in similar small enterprises. He would certainly be unaware of the numerical strength of his "class," and would lack both the means and the inclination to make contact with others in the same type of occupation. The same man in a factory of two thousand workers would be forced to see the gulf between himself and the management. He would begin to think of himself as a "worker" and so begin to listen to messages addressed to the "working classes." The new social structure of the nation further emphasized the class divisions by stressing the importance of each individual's knowing his class. From Jane Austen to H. G. Wells, the novelists of the age depicted, without necessarily approving, a life in which a rigid social stratification was accepted as an axiom of the good society.

Equalitarian democracy appears to be the antithesis of a highly differentiated social class structure. It would, therefore, seem reasonable to expect democracy to restrain the development of group-directed propaganda. But this has not happened. Great Britain and much of continental Europe experienced a raising and strengthening of traditional class barriers in the nineteenth century. On the other side of the Atlantic, the United States became progressively more equalitarian. These two movements, apparently so opposed in spirit, had one thing in common: the rejection of the individual in the name of a larger community. Eventually Europe moved in the same direction as North America, but the gradual breaking down of the class divisions in Victorian England did not lead to any weakening of the type of group thinking which is so important to the propagandist. Indeed, and here I echo de Tocqueville's thoughts on equality in America, the very character of the new democratic society drew each man down behind the shelter of public opinion.

> At periods of equality men have no faith in one another, by reason of their common resemblance; but this very resemblance gives them almost unbounded confidence in the judgement of the public;[1]

The fate of the individual in the mass society seemed grim and unpalatable to such an aristocratic and determined individualist as de Tocqueville, for whom enforced conformity to the standards of the majority would have been an intolerable existence. De Tocqueville's contention was that in a democracy the masses, by their general ignorance and intolerance (which could not be eradicated by the existing standards of education) would tend rather to establish a tyranny than to be guided by reason and justice. The majority raised "very formidable barriers to the liberty of opinion" [2] which, as far as the oppressed individual was concerned, were as intolerable as the restraints imposed by the single tyrant.

The propagandist, who was interested only in results, accepted the trend to conformity in opinion as one of the more useful facts of political life. He began to make practical experiments in the control of the group mind long before the psychologists and sociologists could explain the "why" or "how" of its existence. Indeed it was not until propaganda had established itself as a major force in politics that there was any serious research into the conditions which make it possible. In this process of seeking an explanation for the propagandist's success we must note particularly the work of William McDougall, Graham Wallas, Walter Lippmann, and Wilfred Trotter.[3] McDougall and Wallas were pioneers in the study of the role of instinct and non-rational motivation in human activity and, while it would be out of place here to attempt a summary of their theories, the reader should not ignore them. Of particular importance is Wallas' qualification that while men were to a very large extent governed by "affection and instinct" rather than by reason, only part of their activity, for part of the time, was irrational; and further, it was possible to increase the proportion of rational behavior in men's conduct. This conclusion suggests one limit on the power of propaganda to mold public opinion in any desired fashion.

In *The Great Society* Wallas introduced the word "suggestion," defined as: "the causation of acts, beliefs or feelings by many different processes which are alike only in the negative fact that they are not fully conscious." [4] The actual process of opinion-forming was not, at this stage, important. It was sufficient to recognize that while some of our ideas and actions were based on deliberately logical reasoning, in others reason played a more or less minor role. All the non-rational elements in the second category could be discussed conveniently under the heading of suggestion.

The same term was used later by another English writer, Wilfred Trotter, to distinguish between a rationally and non-rationally formed opinion. Since it was true that irrational belief constituted the bulk of man's opinions and since opinions so formed could not be distinguished by their subject matter from rational, verifiable knowledge, it was useful to have a term such as "suggestion" to distinguish the two processes of opinion-forming. Suggestion in this sense applied to the way in which an opinion was reached and not to the opinion itself. Trotter contributed to the study of propaganda by demonstrating how the deliberate use of suggestion could be a political weapon, especially in regard to that group awareness which was a pre-condition for the development of modern propaganda.

The key lay in the propagandist's realization that he could, through suggestion, exploit to his own advantage the powerful human instinct of gregariousness. The mental fixity and lack of intellectual curiosity that were characteristic of the bulk of mankind were the outcome of man's gregarious instincts. They made the work of the propagandist so much easier by inducing in individuals an intolerance of all non-conformity. Most men were as afraid of mental isolation, of being excluded from the sympathy of other men, as they were of physical solitude. Because of this instinct man became more sensitive to the "voice of the herd" than to any other social influence. The propagandist who spoke "for the people" and who could be accepted by the people as one of themselves had increased his power to stimulate or inhibit thought and conduct. The "tyranny of the majority" feared by J. S. Mill was in this way shaped by Trotter into a guiding principle of propaganda.

The power of suggestion to influence the mental attitudes of men was more easily understandable when it was realized that "man is too anxious to feel certain to have time to know."[5] The determination of the individual to "feel certain" ensured that in wartime, when group consciousness reaches its greatest intensity, the people of every nation would normally believe with an unassailable passion and certitude in the justice of their own cause. The nation at war also provided the most striking example of the power of the "herd instinct" to unify a great number of diverse individuals.[6]

In Italy Gaetano Mosca produced work on substantially the same lines as Trotter, but unfortunately his writings were not available to English readers until 1939. Mosca described how it had become a standard propaganda tactic to portray the independent-minded individual as a dangerous enemy to the unity of the community. The non-conformist who shows signs of thinking for himself can be made to appear guilty of disloyalty, treachery, or sabotage.

Because the "herd instinct" is a characteristic of all human societies, whether democratic or aristocratic, it is as old as society itself, but it is only in recent decades that it has become politically significant. Once the practice of referring certain political decisions to the "herd" had been established, then the control of the "herd" became a matter of some consequence to the politician. For the purpose of the argument here the "herd" consists of any large group of people in whom the propagandist has a direct personal interest whether it be the general membership of a society, an economic class, or the whole population of the state. Even the most skilled propagandist may be a member of the "herd" as far as another propagandist is concerned.

The increasing size, concentration and social stratification of the population, with the consequent stress on conformity, together with the extension of the franchise, brought the problems of public-opinion control to the attention of nineteenth-century political leaders, but certain other factors determined the manner in which the problem should be solved. The first of these emerged directly from the special characteristics of nineteenth-century liberal philosophy, with its emphasis on the responsible individual.

One implication of liberal philosophy was the belief that, once the masses had been taught to read and so to reason, they could be given political power and in fact were entitled, as rational beings, to a share in political life. Belief in such a theory made it difficult to imagine the possibility of the exploitation of an irrational public opinion by ambitious politicians. A semi-dogmatic faith in the ability of egoistic but educated individuals to achieve the objectively good life was scarcely compatible with suggestions that an elementary education might not give every individual either the capacity or the desire for an intelligent participation in social or political activity. Despite the warnings of de Tocqueville and J. S. Mill and the pessimism of Bagehot,[7] a broad faith in the benefits which would follow automatically from the extension of literacy and the franchise to the mass of the people continued to dominate popular thought and writing. The deliberate control of the mass opinion of a literate but otherwise poorly educated and politically immature public was a possibility not at first perceived. Because the liberal philosophers misinterpreted human nature, the institutions they created, although effective in crushing the old tyrannies of aristocrats and kings, prepared the way for the emergence of new tyrannies whose strength lay not in arms but in the support of public opinion.

Democratic liberal political theory and political institutions in an industrial setting were in part responsible for providing the propagandist with an audience ready to receive his attentions. And other conditions, stemming directly from the character of the new society, strengthened the trends it had established. One factor furthering the natural inability of most to determine issues rationally was a lack of interest in politics and a disinclination to acquire the necessary knowledge, a factor which, of course, aided the propagandist who was only too keen to supply the people with the "facts" and opinions they could not get for themselves.

This lack of interest was, in turn, a product of the nineteenth-century cultural environment. In normal circumstances, genuinely creative thought can be achieved only with material comfort, a proper psychological approach to the value of reflective thought, and the development of the necessary faculties. Industrial society, with its poverty, noise and dirt, and its materialistic philosophy, denied these facilities to all but a very small percentage of its citizens. The very nature of a ruthlessly competitive industrial economy made sustained individual reasoning on political questions impossible for the majority of men, including some of those mentally capable of highly intelligent action.

Employers could not allow their workers to discuss social or political problems in the factories or offices; and long hours, heavy work, and the unhealthy, overcrowded dwellings of the working classes did not encourage informal political discussions at home. Those whose incomes permitted them to live in the less intolerable surroundings of the suburbs found that their life there was spent for the most part among strangers, since social customs inhibited easy intercourse among neighbors. When time and opportunity were found for discussion, the materialistic outlook of so many of the prosperous probably did much to ensure that broad social issues would not be introduced into conversation where rigid conventions limited the topics that might be discussed.

As the city worker, both in the office and in the factory, consequently became more and more dependent for his opinions upon the ready-made judgments of the political "experts," there resulted a vast increase in the amount of uncritical reading—a trend accentuated by the rise of cheap, mass-circulation newspapers. The social fabric of the state provided the propagandist with an audience ready and willing to receive the message he was now, for the first time, technically equipped to deliver.[8]

THE MEANS OF COMMUNICATION

The propagandist required, in addition to a demand for his work and an audience capable of receiving it, the physical means of carrying his material to his audience. Here was one of the supreme achievements of the nineteenth century. The age of modern communications began in

1825 with the opening of the Stockton and Darlington Railway in England, the first strand in a vast network of railroads which "symbolised the conquest of space and parochialism." [9] Apart from the purely economic advantages of the cheaper and more rapid movement of a great quantity and variety of goods, and the opening up of hitherto inaccessible territories, the railways had important political effects for the development of propaganda. As more people traveled more often and farther, the concept of nation took a firmer hold in the public mind. For centuries in England the man from the next county had been almost as much a foreigner as the man from China. The citizens of Morlaix or St. Brieuc would think of themselves as Bretons first and only secondly as Frenchmen; they would feel little in common with the Parisians they would never have occasion to meet. The railways played a major part in breaking down this isolation of peoples, welding the fragmentary pieces into a unified whole. Local dialects, traditions, and cultures may have suffered, but the nation and the sense of national patriotism were immeasurably strengthened.

The technical revolution thus did two things. It made the formation of nationwide groups easier and facilitated communication between members of such groups, and at the same time it strengthened the nation itself as a single group in the community of nations. Writing on Germany for example, Heaton described how the "railroad knit her together politically and economically and made the Empire a reality. It also knit her into the fabric of continental Europe, with strands that stretched westward to the North Sea and the English Channel, eastward into Russia, and southward to Austria, Italy and Constantinople." [10] In the first flush of the railway age, the old coaching roads sank into decline. Their later rebuilding and extension with the invention of the automobile changed the pace, but not the character, of the movement begun by the railroads. In North America in particular the cheap mass-produced automobile has given to millions a knowledge and awareness of their nation that they could never otherwise have acquired. A land as vast as the United States tends always to split into distinct political, economic and cultural regions. The effects of this tendency are clearly visible as one travels from say, New England to the Middle West, but there is a powerful counter-agent in the automobile and in the willingness of the American to travel thousands of miles a year in search of change and variety. It would be only a slight exaggeration to suggest that the automobile had been the major force in strengthening and preserving American national unity.

Further opportunities for the rapid and efficient spread of ideas came with the establishment of cheap, nationwide postal services. A whole new field of communication was opened up; a field that, with the spread of literacy, became increasingly significant. As it was set up in each country in turn, the new postal system had an immediate and far-reaching effect, for with it the propagandist acquired the means to reach quickly and inexpensively practically every member of the community.

In any account of modern communications the press must be given special attention, for of all propaganda media the press is the most firmly established and the most widely used. It is only now that its predominance is being challenged by the radio and television. Where the press had once been important only to an intellectual minority, a series of technical inventions and Parliamentary Acts in the nineteenth century made possible its evolution as a powerful instrument of mass communication.

A detailed history of the modern press is out of place here, for it is a lengthy story and one which has been told many times before.[11] A series of inventions made possible newspaper circulations running into millions. These inventions were in turn the product of an increased demand for newspapers from the newly-educated public. But before the people would in fact buy the newspapers which could now be produced and sold so cheaply, it was necessary to write what the people would want to read. Some of the "giants" of the press world were quick to realize this. The modern press in Britain and in America is to a very large

extent a reflection of the work of a few dominant personalities who saw how the spread of literacy had created an
enormous potential reading public and who molded their
papers to appeal to the widest possible audience. In
America, Joseph Pulitzer and William Randolph Hearst,
in Britain, the Lords Northcliffe and Beaverbrook, set the
style which has been imitated by all men seeking a cheap
and effective method of appealing to popular opinion.

A more modern development which modifies the full
freedom of discussion supposedly characteristic of democracy had been the enormous increase in newspaper
circulations, combined with a decline in the total number
of papers and the concentration of the survivors in fewer
hands. Thus, in the United States, the total circulation of
daily newspapers rose from 27 million in 1920 to nearly
58 million in 1957, while the number of daily newspapers
declined from a peak of 2,502 in 1915 to 1,755 in 1957.[12]

The mass-circulation newspapers created a habit of reading which soon came to demand a more varied diet for its
satisfaction. In the past fifty years there has been an enormous and still-accelerating increase in the production of
all kinds of printed material—books, magazines, pamphlets
and learned journals—all of which can, of course, be part
of the propagandist's media of communication.

Just as distance had been conquered by mechanical
improvements, so time, another obstacle to the spread of
ideas, was eventually overcome, first by the telegraph and
telephone, and later by radio and television. These last two,
although eventually they were to become the greatest of
all media of mass communication, took longer to establish,
and, although the principles of wireless communication had
been successfully demonstrated in the first decade of the
century, it was not until the 1920's that popular radio
programs were broadcast for the benefit of the general
public. The subsequent development was astonishingly
rapid and today radio and the still more recent television
have become part of the normal life of most people in the
industrialized countries. There are few people in Western
Europe or North America who cannot, if they wish, gain

easy access to either a radio or a television receiver. Indeed, it seems not unlikely that among those who do not have radios, poverty is less often the reason than is a conscious determination not to own a set, motivated perhaps by religious or esthetic principles, or simply the cultivation of non-conformity.

When the speed of communication was tied to that of a galloping horse, the governments of ancient empires had but limited control over their more distant outposts. So long as it took many weeks for reports and instructions to pass from the colonial to the central government and back again, the local commander could assume wide discretionary power. Now a revolution in communication, beginning with the railways and ending with broadcasting, had conquered both time and space. Official reports, orders, information and encouragement could be passed instantaneously to the farthest-flung corners of the realm. For the first time governments, and those who aspired to government, had both the need and means to communicate quickly with ordinary people. The propagandist had thus at least a potential influence as great as that possessed by any ancient despot.

The Influence of Advertising

The tremendous volume of energy unleashed by the discovery of the steam engine brought to the world markets a flood of consumer goods. Throughout the nineteenth century, men became obsessed with the frenzied process of turning raw materials into finished goods. All manner of metals, clay, sand, coal, cotton, and wool were delivered to the industrial areas to return as machinery, pots, bathtubs, ships, fabrics, iron railings, and plate glass. Articles for factory, city, street, home, and individual were turned out in a bewildering, unprecedented, and often senseless profusion. But when production outpaced demand, as it so often did, new demands had to be created to absorb the surplus. In the consequent atmosphere of merciless competition, accentuated by the prevailing economic philos-

ophy, the existence of the individual manufacturer de-
pended upon his ability to outsell his rivals. Industrialists,
as well as retailers, became more and more concerned with
the highly specialized and increasingly difficult task of
selling the goods they could now so easily produce. Commercial advertising, the art of selling goods, like the art
of selling ideas, became a characteristic feature of life in
the competitive industrial society.[13]

As publicity and advertising became increasingly significant, closer and more specialized attention was given to
the study of technique and method. Advertisers discovered
the power of the non-rational, the appeal of novelty, the
force of repetition, and the need for simplicity. Necessity
compelled advertisers to develop the most effective process
for presenting an idea in a form in which it would be seen,
understood, remembered, and acted upon. Many modern
writers have linked the development of propaganda with
the parallel development of advertising. It is quite clear that
propagandists have learned much from the commercial
advertisers and, indeed, most of the examples in the
earliest studies of modern propaganda technique were
drawn from commercial experience.[14] Those with goods to
sell made the first experiments with each new form of
advertising; posters and trademarks, which are the direct
descendants of the banners of the medieval guilds; symbols
for the unlettered, such as the pawnbroker's three golden
balls, the barber's striped pole, and the pharmacist's mortar
and pestle; bulletins, newsletters, printing in all its forms—
all these things were used to sell goods long before they
were used for any systematic large-scale selling of ideas.

> In the modern world advertising is the oldest form of
> propaganda. It has developed concurrently with the rise
> of the press and the expansion of commerce; and most of
> the methods employed by the propagandist in other fields
> today, especially in politics, are but devices borrowed from
> commercial advertising.[15]

So much is obvious, but there is another aspect that has
not been so well understood. The advertiser, in order to
make his message stand out in a highly competitive society,

was compelled to adopt the most spectacular attention-getting practices. In time, practical experiment in advertising techniques came to be supplemented by professional training in business methods. In the schools, however, writers on selling methods, in order to illustrate their arguments most effectively, concentrated on the best-known, most successful, or most original advertising. They tended thereby to over emphasize the irrational and the spectacular and so to imply, perhaps unintentionally, that all advertising consisted of slogans, exaggerations, half-truths and suggestions.

It is true that these techniques are widely used in advertising, but is it not true that they are necessary for the existence of advertising, nor that they are the only form of advertising. Advertising, which is basically a process of inducing people to buy goods, is often irrational, blatant and vulgar, but this is not the same thing as saying that advertising is an irrational, blatant and vulgar process for inducing people to buy goods. The confusion of advertising, or propaganda, with one particular unpleasant manifestation of advertising, or propaganda, has led many to a confusion that has important consequences when one is trying to understand the place of propaganda in a democratic society. Although the development and techniques of propaganda and advertising are clearly involved with each other, it has often been contended that the two are mutually exclusive forms of persuasion. William Albig, for example, first in his *Public Opinion* (1939) and later in his *Modern Public Opinion* (1956) put forward the thesis that the source of propaganda is always concealed. It was essentially a secret, underhand business, for once the identity of the promoter was revealed, his activity became simply advertising.

> Advertising may be distinguished from propaganda in that the sources of the advertisement are stated and the motives of the advertiser may be readily assumed (when the sources are concealed, as in the case of a food-products company publicizing its claims over the name of a supposed scientific research organization, we have commercial propaganda).[16]

There does not appear to be any justification for this attitude and, as we have already shown, the idea of concealed propaganda leads into many serious difficulties and contradictions. A more satisfactory approach is to accept the undoubted similarity between propaganda and advertising and to regard them as essentially the same thing—a process for inducing people to make certain decisions about goods or ideas. The two expressions "advertising" and "propaganda" then become simply conventional and often overlapping terms for distinguishing the commercial and political aspects of a single phenomenon. This point was made some years ago by H. C. Brown in a paper in which he wrote that propaganda and advertising should be considered together, for although the latter was concerned with the sale of goods for somebody's profit, propaganda was really nothing more than the sale of ideas, perhaps ostensibly for the common good, but usually also for somebody's profit.[17]

To treat propaganda and advertising in this way rescues one from the logical problems that arise when attempting to give advertising a higher ethical value than propaganda, and it avoids any problems of classification in those many cases where a great deal of political content can be found in a commercial advertisement. This last point is particularly interesting for, in the advertising of many large corporations which lend their prestige and name to certain "public-service" campaigns, politics and business are inseparable. One particularly notable example of an advertisement of this kind appeared in the special Coronation issue of *Picture Post* on June 6, 1953. The text is well worth quoting here.

To you, the People of Britain, our natural partners in the cause of Peace and Trade, our comrades in time of war, and our cousins by blood and heritage, WE, the men and women of THE NATIONAL CASH REGISTER COMPANY in the United States of America, extend the firm hand of Friendship—that, on the Great Occasion of Your Rejoicing, we may clasp it with Yours in the True Spirit of a neighbour's Greeting—aware, as forever we shall be,

that in the destinies of our two Nations, nothing can divide
us but the sea.
GOD BLESS QUEEN ELIZABETH II.
(signed) S. G. ALLYRING President.
Makers of Accounting Machines, Adding Machines & Cash
Registers to Commerce, Industry, Finance & Governments
Throughout the World.

Besides being propaganda for an Anglo-American alliance,
this is certainly a superb piece of prestige copy for the
National Cash Register Company. It is probably not possible to frame a definition which would make a final and
absolute separation of these two aspects of publicity.

THE GROWING AWARENESS
OF PROPAGANDA

The social, economic, and political forces released in
the nineteenth century by the combined efforts of liberal
philosophy, the growth of industrial cities, and a vastly
increased population brought into prominence a phenomenon we now call propaganda. Unfortunately, the novelty
and spectacular natures of certain methods adopted by the
propagandists led observers to confuse these methods with
the nature of propaganda as such. This inability to distinguish between propaganda and certain restricted mani-
festations of propaganda had serious consequences on later
attempts to understand the process of public-opinion control. The problem became particularly important after the
experience of the First World War had aroused wide public
interest in the subject.

The immediate question to consider is how political
scientists first came to consider the significance of this new
factor in social life. One of the first to realize that the
existence of propaganda did demand some re-thinking of
the bases for democracy was B. Jerrold in a paper published
in 1883.[18] Jerrold's thesis was that as public opinion,
through the extension of the suffrage, had become the
"motive power by which ministries are sustained and over-
thrown" it was essential to examine more closely "the

manufacture of public opinion." This was an art that, having "remained long in infancy" had now attained a new prominence and significance. Jerrold was well aware of the threat to the liberal concept of democracy implicit in the growing power of the "public opinion manufacturer," with his newly-developed techniques of publicity and persuasion. There was a definite possibility that through propaganda men might acquire the power to "weaken and pollute representative systems at their base" while leaving their form and appearance unchanged.

In the last twenty years of the nineteenth century, political commentators began to appreciate the fact that universal suffrage would not solve all mankind's problems. A few years earlier de Tocqueville and J. S. Mill had warned of the "tyranny of the majority"; now it seemed that ways had been discovered for the few to impose their mind on the majority and to use the weight of the majority against any opposition. The tyranny of the few would be perpetuated, but it would have the appearance of the will of the majority. It was with a somewhat similar theme in mind that S. Kydd wrote in 1888:

> When power is lodged in an assembly elected by popular suffrage, political speculation and mendacious orators may exercise greater influence than despots, kings, or ruling families have done.[19]

By the turn of the present century it was clear that the machinery of representative government was not working as smoothly as its liberal creators had intended. As the gulf between the theory and the practice of democracy became more obvious there resulted a widespread disillusionment which led many to a complete rejection of the democratic thesis. This was the setting that had encouraged Ostrogorski, Michels and others to prophesy the collapse of democratic liberal machinery, and it was within this same framework that Graham Wallas wrote *Human Nature in Politics*. Wallas recognized that there was throughout Europe a widespread dissatisfaction with the day-to-day application of democratic theory. In place of such democratic concepts as liberty, equality, reason, and government by the people—dismissed now as mere shibboleths—new schools of thought demanded a more "realistic" approach to government based on the observable facts of human conduct. Too often, unfortunately, the "observable facts" were no more than a simple contradiction of earlier faiths.

Wallas saw how a "realistic reaction of this kind could be as false and as dangerous as the still-popular intellectual dogmatism of the nineteenth century. As a realist himself, he knew the weakness of certain democratic premises, but he denied the validity of the anti-democrats' conclusions. While preserving his faith in democracy, he sought to base it on firmer foundations, first of all by explaining the fallacies of the traditional democratic approach, and secondly by suggesting ways of overcoming the difficulties which arose from those fallacies. The founders of democratic theory were undoubtedly right in believing they had discovered the means for a fuller expression of human dignity and a more complete development of the individual's potential, but their uncritical overemphasis on the role of reason in political activity had made impossible the realization of their ideal through the machinery they had established, especially the machinery for the election of representatives. The creators of the existing parliamentary institutions, said Wallas,[20] had started from a purely intellectual and undeniably false concept of human nature: "The assumption . . . that men always act on a reasoned opinion as to their interest." (p. 98) This assumption had to be abandoned if man was to set his democracy on more substantial foundations. "Whoever sets himself to base his political thinking on a re-examination of the working of human nature, must begin by trying to overcome his own tendency to exaggerate the intellectuality of mankind." (p. 21)

From his conclusion that men were not entirely governed by reason, but often acted on "affection and instinct," Wallas developed the further idea that perhaps such "affection and instinct" could be deliberately aroused and directed in a way that would eventually lead to some course of action desired by the manipulator. Wallas was not the first to realize that the vote-catching techniques of the professional politicians might threaten the successful working of representative democracy. He was, however, one of the first to see modern electioneering practices as a reflection of the character of human nature in a particular institutional framework. Given a greatly expanded franchise, with its corollary of the need to base authority on the support of public opinion, political society invited the attention of the professional controller of public opinion. When to the demand for new methods of publicity there were added revolutionary advances in the techniques of communication and the latest discoveries in social psychology, mankind had to fear more than ever "the cold-blooded manipulation of popular impulse and thought by professional politicians." (p. 201)

The importance of psychology to an understanding of politics has been treated at length by many writers from the time of Freud until the present day. However, for the period covered by this chapter, the most important contribution to the subject, with particular reference to propaganda, was probably that of Walter Lippmann. Writing first in *A Preface to Politics* (1913), and later in *Public Opinion* (1922), Lippmann discussed the application of the techniques and discoveries of the psychologist to political science.

While what Lippmann termed the "creation of consent" was as old as politics, modern propaganda had succeeded in developing methods of scientific analysis in place of simple experience, intuition, and trial-and-error innovation. When the discoveries of psychological research and the enormously improved means of communication were combined with this scientific approach, there resulted a revolution in the practice of democracy, a revolution "infinitely more significant than any shifting in economic power." Within the lifetime of those then in control of affairs, "persuasion had become a self-conscious art" and a "regular organ of popular government." The knowledge of how to create consent had profoundly altered every political calculation and "modified every political premise" to an extent none could yet pretend to understand. Already it was impossible to accept the original dogma of democracy that the knowledge needed to control human affairs came up "spontaneously from the human heart." To act on that theory now was to risk self-deception and exposure to "forms of persuasion" that could not be verified. Under the impact of propaganda it had been proved that men could no longer rely on "intuition, conscience, or the accidents of casual opinion" if they were to deal with the world around them.[21]

As part of his investigation into the character of public opinion Lippmann introduced the useful term "stereotype" to describe the knowledge men thought they had about things: knowledge based on myths, dreams, and so on, as distinct from genuine knowledge.[22] Like Sorel,[23] who may have influenced him, Lippmann believed in the power of the myth or stereotype to arouse popular enthusiasm. He knew that abstract ideas, feelings of national, local or racial pride, glory in ancient traditions, personal wishes, and popular passions are more real to the great mass of the people than are actual realities. The role of the myth in politics is often overlooked in democratic theory, yet it is of fundamental importance to the propagandist. Because the myth is intangible, it is easier to mold than fact, although it is still as real as life itself to those who believe in it. Some of the Fascists later came to have a startling insight into the meaning of the myth as an instrument of political control, although it should not be assumed that myths are an exclusively Fascist phenomenon. To quote Mussolini: "The myth is a faith, it is passion. It is not necessary that it shall be a reality. It is a reality by the fact that it is a goad, a hope, a faith, that it is courage." [24] For the propagandist, the myth is the most important form of the stereotype. It is impossible to understand the success of propaganda without also understanding how great a part of what men regard as knowledge is in fact no more than a collection of stereotypes.

The development of propaganda, both as a factor in political life and as an object of academic study, had reached a relatively advanced stage by the turn of the present century. There was still, however, little popular awareness of the importance, or even the possibility, of mass public-opinion control. The awakening of public concern in propaganda was one of the consequences of the war of 1914-1918. The influence of this war on modern concepts of propaganda will be taken up in the next chapter.

Three

PROPAGANDA AT WAR

When in the twentieth century the traditional armies of the mercenaries were replaced by national armies, the individual citizen had as never before a personal interest in the outcome of war. Wars were now between nations and not merely between armies. In the new kind of war the unprecedented consumption of munitions and other materials demanded the recruiting of the civilian populations and the mobilization of the entire economic resources of the state. Women were asked to work in the munition factories, to nurse the sick, and to take over the jobs left by the men who went to war. The manufacture of civilian luxuries was halted, food was rationed, raw materials were controlled and directed to war production. All things became subservient to that one end of winning the war.

With the nation at war, appeals to national pride and loyalty took on a new and deeper meaning, giving men a courage to fight on and a purpose in death. As Bertrand Russell [1] has observed, a nation which was to succeed in modern war had to be able to convince its people that the cause of victory was worthy of martyrdom. But because the call of patriotism would be answered only if the people believed in their identity as a nation and recognized the war as their war, governments recruited experts to take over the ideological side of the conflict. It came to be recognized that influencing men's minds was another important theater of conflict, as essential to victory as the production of guns, the healing of the sick, and the destruction of the enemy's property. Then, as aircraft carried the war behind the front lines, civilians began to share the dangers of the fighting forces. But civilians could do little to fight back, and lacked that discipline and unity of purpose that can help a soldier conquer fear. Propaganda, and especially emotive propaganda, was therefore adopted as a substitute for discipline to carry the nation through crises and to mold it into a single organized fighting unit.

The importance of propaganda was not, of course, recognized at once. Although an increasing number of political scientists were becoming aware of the possibilities of propaganda, few outside this specialist field were familiar with it. In 1914, for example, it was still thought that the war would be "over by Christmas," so long-term propaganda planning would have been a foolish waste of time and energy. The first experiments in propaganda on the Allied side came therefore from unofficial organizations. Governments and military leaders began to take an interest only when they realized the frightening cost of victory in terms of men, materials and suffering; when anything which might lessen the cost was worth trying. The gradual building up of the British and American propaganda services indicated the growing strength of this aspect of the war. It is beyond the scope of this present work to detail the development of official propaganda agencies from what had at first been the purely voluntary work of patriotic individuals. The interested reader is referred to a very extensive literature in this field. A selection of the most important titles will be found in the bibliography at the end of this book.

PROPAGANDA AND POLICY

As the war continued and ideological issues took on a deeper significance, propaganda ceased to be a matter for enthusiastic amateurs. It was realized that some form of cooperation in the propaganda programs of the Allies would be more effective than uncoördinated activities, no matter how well conducted. Therefore, in February, 1918, Lord Northcliffe, in charge of British propaganda against

Germany, called a conference in London to consolidate the propaganda policies of the Allied Powers. Representatives from Great Britain, the United States, France, and Italy attended. As no official record of this conference seems to be available I have summarized the account of the proceedings from the description in H. W. Steed's autobiography.[2]

In writing of the Inter-Allied Propaganda Conference, Steed drew special attention to a speech by a member of the French delegation, M. Henri Moysset, which set out the basis for a systematic Allied propaganda policy. This, said Steed, was the first serious definition of propaganda to be formulated in any Allied country. The Allies, said Moysset, were to begin "a war of ideas against Germany as a corollary of military resistance to her attack." He went on to say that Germany had made the idea of war acceptable to her own people by "a generation of sedulous propaganda." [3] "Military defeat would not necessarily entail political defeat for Germany unless she were also beaten in the realm of ideas."

In view of the military position Moysset suggested that the Allied propaganda should first aim at quick results and then at the transformation of the state of mind prevailing in the countries allied to Germany, rather than in Germany itself. Allied propaganda should therefore be directed primarily against Austria-Hungary and "should be based on the aspirations of the subject Hapsburg races." Here enemy morale was at its lowest and disruptive-revolutionary and defeatist propaganda would be most likely to succeed. Only when the solidarity of the enemy's alliance began to crumble would it be practical to attack Germany directly. Moysset recalled how, in the early days of the war, the Allies had held Germany responsible for the conflict, but by 1918 they appeared to have abandoned this theme. This, he said, was a mistake and the Allies should develop German responsibility for the war as a leading feature of their propaganda. They should insist that after the war "Germans and Austro-Hungarians would have to face moral ostracism in a civilized world until atonement had been

made." The ideological aspect of the war would be strengthened if it could be shown that "Prussianism constituted a
moral anachronism in the modern world."

But propaganda cannot remain destructive. It is not
enough to undermine the moral strength of the enemy without offering something in its place. Therefore, Moysset proposed that the Allies should confront the Germans "with
a positive formulation of public right and of the Law of
Nations superior to the German conception of *Kultur*."
The attempt to define and clarify these ideas would compel
the Allies to frame a positive conception of the future
political and moral reconstruction of Europe, and to make
up their minds as to the place of Germany in a recon-
structed Europe. Thus they would have to put before neutrals and before the German people a forecast of the position which Germany would hold; and they would compel
the German people to consider whether it would be worth
while to continue the war, with all its perils, for the sake
of a problematical mastery over Europe and the World." [4]

Moysset at this stage was expressing a point of view
shared by many other leading Allied propagandists: the
idea that the duties of the propagandist went further even
than the presentation of the Allied policy to the enemy and
to neutrals. In his view, policy should be initially formulated in consultation with the propagandists, who could
then consider not only the immediate objectives of that
policy, but also the effects of its publication on home and
foreign opinion. While it was not suggested that policy
should be so flexible that principles counted for nothing, it
was desirable that policy should be so expressed that it
would bring about the most favorable attitudes among
enemies, neutrals and allies.

From this approach, propaganda, embracing the ideas
behind the entire moral and political reconstruction of Europe becomes something far removed from the popular
concept of it as a matter of hysterical speeches and surrender leaflets. For Moysset, as for Lord Northcliffe, the
basic policy of the Allies, both for the prosecution of the
war and for the settlement afterwards, had its propaganda

value and should be formulated with some regard to its propaganda functions. This broad concept of propaganda has in this present age been even further expanded into a combined political, economic, military and psychological campaign termed "psychological warfare."

The Allied political and military leaders came slowly to realize that their postwar policy could indeed be used as a weapon of war. President Wilson, for example, by virtue of what Harold Lasswell called "his monumental rhetoric, epitomizing the aspirations of all humanity" became one of the greatest propagandists of history. For years Wilson had been ridiculed and caricatured throughout Germany, but as the German military machine began to collapse, Wilson appeared as the "last desperate hope of the defeated peoples for a soft peace." His "seductive voice" undermined German unity, fomented discord in the enemy's ranks and restored hope and courage to the conquered. As Lasswell said, men will long debate "just how much of Wilsonism was rhetorical exhibitionism and how much was the sound fruit of sober reflection," but all of it was superb propaganda.[5] Wilson, more than anyone else, gave the war its special character as "the war to end war." This slogan had a peculiarly heartening effect on the Allies for it rationalized the awful sordidness and slaughter of war into something which had as its object the noblest of ends— lasting peace. In the next war Dr. Goebbels paid further tribute to the impact of Wilson's program for peace.[6]

Truth in Wartime Propaganda

Since the war, propaganda has been popularly associated with falsehood and for many it is a contradiction to refer to truthful propaganda. But while it may be difficult to find examples of propaganda that tell the truth, the whole truth, and nothing but the truth, it is not impossible. It is a task that becomes easier once there is agreement on the nature of truth.

The propagandist is anxious to bring about certain results. He is successful if people act as he wishes them to act, and even more successful if they do so apparently of their own free will. He will try to use such material and techniques as are available and that seem most likely to lead to the desired state of affairs. In normal circumstances, a completely impartial presentation of all relevant material will be contrary to the propagandist's interests, and therefore the truth is often abandoned. Nevertheless, there are also many circumstances where the propagandist's objectives can best be achieved by strict adherence to the truth, and in these conditions the truth is employed. The attempted persuasion is no less propaganda because it is based on truth.

At the time of the First World War the practicing propagandists of the day saw no contradiction in speaking of truthful propaganda, and it was only in the 1930's that political scientists tried, albeit in vain, to use truth as a criterion for distinguishing propaganda and education. Indeed, the war propagandists took considerable pains to make it clear that as far as they were concerned, truth and propaganda were the same thing. Their faith in their own virtue, made quite clear by the following quotations, was not always substantiated by the evidence, but the point to be made here is that those engaged in propaganda saw no reason why it should not be truthful propaganda. This is what some of them had to say on the matter. "The first of all axioms of propaganda is that only truthful statements be made." [7] "From the first, Crewe House propaganda had been based upon truth—truth as to policy, truth as to facts, truth as to intentions. Lying propaganda defeats itself sooner or later." [8] A maxim of Crewe House "was to tell the enemy the plain truth, and nothing but the truth, without *suggestio falsi* or deft interpretation." [9] "It is the pride of the Committee, as it should be the pride of America, that every activity was at all times open to the sun." [10] "Our information did not consist of lies, misstatements, half-truths or exaggerations." [11]

The Allied propagandists, in writing of their exploits, were able to prove that at least a great deal of their material was factually true. They described how they had announced to the Allied peoples news of casualties, of food shortages, of ships sunk, and of battles lost. They gave the enemy accurate figures of American industrial production and of enemy casualties. One of the most widely-used forms of propaganda against the enemy soldier was the leaflet dropped over his lines, showing him, in a simple sketch map, the latest advances of the Allied troops. It was essential for the success of this type of propaganda that no false claims be made. The files in the Imperial War Museum in London and in the Hoover War Library at Stanford contain copies of leaflets dropped by the Allies over German lines. These concentrate on such topics as a comparison of food rations in Britain and in Germany, the increasing number of American soldiers landing in Europe, the rising cost of living in Germany, or the increasing production of grain in the United States and Canada. All such statistics, and particularly those which the enemy might himself be able to verify, were substantially correct. Indeed, much of the remarkable success of the Allied propaganda was the result of a basic adherence to facts. Because it was difficult to pinpoint deliberate falsehoods, the Allied propagandists could gain the confidence of their audience. The propaganda was received because it had about it an air of truth.

Practicing propagandists have in fact always recognized that even when it is not opportune to tell the whole truth, at least what is said should be factually true. Hitler's doctrine of the "big lie" is applicable only in the closed environment of the authoritarian state where the positive programs of the propagandist are reinforced by a rigid censorship excluding all competitive propaganda. Even then, experience showed the lie to be less effective propaganda than Hitler imagined. In the ordinary day-to-day propaganda campaigns, outright misrepresentations of fact are too easily discovered to be safe material and the successful propagandist resorts to lying only when the truth is even more dangerous to his cause.

For the most part, therefore, propaganda lying consists of omissions, which are less difficult to justify or excuse, rather than deliberate misrepresentations. Censorship which, by excluding some facts, gives a different weight or value to those which are released, becomes in this way a form of positive propaganda. It is interesting here to consult the Chief British Naval Censor of the First World War, Sir Douglas Brownrigg.[12] Brownrigg was, by his own account, impressed with the value of truth in propaganda, and seems to have devoted much of his energy to the relaxation of censorship regulations against the opposition of his military superiors. His attitude appears in his account of what he called the *Audacious* incident. This British battleship had been sunk in October, 1914, but although this fact seems to have been widely known, the news of the loss was officially withheld from the public until after the war. In Brownrigg's opinion the continued suppression of the news greatly weakened the confidence of the public at home and in neutral countries. It also provided the Germans with useful propaganda against the Allies.[13]

There are, of course, more ways of telling a lie than simply by distorting the facts or imposing censorship. Indeed, before going further it may be worthwhile to examine Arthur Ponsonby's comments on the various forms a propaganda lie can take.[14]

There is, first of all, what is normally understood by a lie, "the deliberate official lie, issued either to delude the people at home, or to mislead the enemy abroad," which is the direct assertion of something known to be untrue. When the Allied propagandists later claimed that they had told only the truth, this is the sort of falsehood they were denying. "The hysterical hallucinations" of weak-minded individuals and organizations could be a form of lying if officialdom, discreetly approving their effect, made no attempt to counteract them. Here the official propagandists could claim that they always spoke the truth and it was no concern of theirs that others lied. Ponsonby, however, argued that deliberately to leave a lie uncorrected was in itself a form of lying.

A completely false impression could be created through a poor translation of foreign documents and papers. Even an otherwise accurate translation could mislead if no allowance was made for idiom or for variations in the usage of a term. The word propaganda itself illustrates this point, for it has, in English speaking countries, a connotation of sinister, unethical behavior. To the Italian, however, it has no such implication, and the Italian propagandist feels no obligation to dress up his activities under some such label as "public relations," or "mass communication." More recently, when the Russians spoke of the genial Stalin, Western propagandists commented acidly on the submissiveness of a people who could accept the absurd proposition that the dour authoritarian was a friendly, affable fellow. For the Russians, however, "genial" was an adjective drawn from the noun "genius" and was intended to refer to Stalin's supposed extraordinary learning and ability.

Deliberate forgeries were used by all the belligerents, but to be effective or foolproof they had to be skillfully manufactured. Generally, they were felt to be a dangerous form of propaganda to be used only as a last resort. Faked or carefully-posed photographs were more common. A widely-used form of this involved pictures of smiling, well-clad groups of prisoners of war quietly relaxing in the sun, eating enormous meals, playing chess or listening to music. The Allies dropped thousands of these over the enemy front lines. The same form of propaganda was used again with some success in the Second World War where it was intended to contrast the discomforts and dangers of the fighting front with the security and relative comfort of the prison camp. But experience demonstrated the futility of exaggerating the comforts of the prison camps, or even of telling the full truth when relating actual (but to the Germans improbable) stories of prisoners in America being given eggs for breakfast. Later, as the Allied forces learned by experience, they gave their propaganda an added point with the highly effective slogan: "Better Free than a Prisoner of War: Better a Prisoner of War than Dead!"

Another form of lying exists in the failure of the authorities to take action to counter the flood of personal accusations and false charges made in the prejudiced war atmosphere to discredit persons refusing to adopt the orthodox attitudes. To allow hysterical nationalism to appear as the only form of patriotism is to practice deceit.

Finally, there is slander of the enemy; "the repetition of a single instance of cruelty, and its exaggeration, can be distorted into a prevailing habit on the part of the enemy."

One may reject as inaccurate and prejudiced certain extreme attacks on the honesty of the war propagandists. Garnett's view that "Crewe House and its foreign equivalents lied like troopers or, to be exact, lied instead of trooping" and lied "more systematically and more effectively than any troopers," is itself a prejudiced and one-sided example of propaganda against propagandists.[15] Yet, while such articles do give a distorted image of the work of the wartime propagandists, and while most of these propagandists did make frequent and honest use of truthful material, it is also true that all the major powers at some time resorted to the various forms of lying in their wartime propaganda.

In all the major studies of wartime propaganda there are numerous authenticated examples of deliberately false propaganda circulated by the Allies. The following incident, for example, is included among several quoted by Bruntz. On March 28, 1918, the *Daily Bulletin* published by Creel's Committee on Public Information contained photographs of the building and shipment of aircraft to France. According to the story in the *Bulletin,* the aircraft, which were the "acme of engineering art," were ready for shipment to France; hundreds had already been sent and the factories were in the stage of quantity production; "thousands and thousands would soon follow." In truth, the photographs had been taken at the factory. They were of parts not yet ready for shipment and only one plane had so far been sent to France.[16] Another incident recounted by Lasswell concerns a picture which appeared in a London newspaper in 1915. The caption read, "Three German cavalrymen loaded with gold and silver loot." It was, however, a "defaced reproduction of a picture which had originally appeared in the *Berliner Lokalanzeiger*" in June 1914, showing the winners of a cavalry competition with their cups and trophies.[17]

IRRATIONAL PROPAGANDA

Just as many writers have seen propaganda as something identical with falsehood, many others have assumed that all propaganda is essentially irrational. This is not an entirely arbitrary standpoint for there is a great deal of evidence to support it. Human attitudes are based on many influences, including instincts, biological urges, spiritual aspirations and a complex range of psychological impulses. A propaganda campaign that is to succeed in changing popular attitudes has to appeal therefore to the non-rational motives governing those attitudes; but, insofar as our attitudes are also the product of rational decision, propaganda must appeal to the rational elements of human nature..

In short, propaganda must be adjusted to suit the audience for which it is intended. It may often be rational, but strictly rational propaganda will be effective only to the extent that the audience is also rational. The propagandist who is trying to reach the largest possible audience and to convert it in the shortest possible time will therefore find it expedient to appeal to the lowest intellectual level, which means that most propaganda is directed towards the more easily controllable irrational motivations. In all ages the propagandists who have achieved fame or notoriety have recognized the inadequacy of purely rational argument in mass appeals.

Some propaganda indeed, especially that created in the tense emotional atmosphere of a nation at war, is so exceedingly irrational that, studied in calmer times, it is difficult to envisage a state of mind that could accept it. In the war of 1914-18 one of the most extreme examples of irrational propaganda was the following:

Credo For France

I believe in the courage of our soldiers and in the skill and devotion of our leaders. I believe in the power of right and the crusade of civilization, in France, the eternal, the imperishable, the essential. I believe in the reward of suffering and in the worth of hope. I believe in confidence, in quiet thought, in the humble daily round, in discipline, in charity militant. I believe in the blood of wounds and the water of benediction; in the blaze of artillery and the flame of the votive candle; in the beads of the rosary. I believe in the hallowed vows of the old, and in the potent innocence of children. I believe in women's prayers, in the helpless heroism of the wife, in the calm piety of the mother, in the purity of our cause, in the stainless glory of our flag. I believe in our great past, in our great present, and in our great future. I believe in our countrymen, living and dead. I believe in the hands clenched for battle, and in the hands clasped for prayer. I believe in ourselves, I believe in God. I believe, I believe.[18]

This, while a rather extreme outburst of patriotic sentiment, is not too far from the spirit of the national songs of many otherwise sophisticated and civilized nations. The collected national anthems of the United Nations illustrate a few simple themes: the military might of each nation, its tradition of liberty, and its especially favored place in the esteem of the Almighty.

Propaganda is not, of course, simply an affair of leaflets and songs, and, if a survey of propaganda techniques is extended to include a wider range of activities, the possible variation of emotional content becomes obvious. Such a study demonstrates that extreme irrationality is only one form of propaganda and is not necessarily the most successful form.

Thus, in order to impress the Germans with British progress in industry, particularly in those fields in which Germany excelled before the war, catalogues of the Scientific Exhibition held in London in 1918 were smuggled into Germany. This sort of propaganda, unemotional in content, was directed to a particular limited audience who would remain unmoved by the cruder appeals addressed to the common soldiers, but who might be deeply disturbed at the possible loss of postwar markets. Then for other specialized audiences the allied propagandists prepared intelligent and reasoned surveys of European history and culture and produced academic studies of political and social theory. This material was propaganda because it was used as such by men determined on winning the war, but in its content it was also quite objective and rational.

One particular form of irrational propaganda that becomes especially important in wartime is atrocity propaganda—the attempt to instill hatred and contempt for the enemy, or perhaps fear and consequently a heightened determination to resist his advances, by recounting his barbarous behavior. In the First World War such a large part of propaganda material, both Allied and German, was made up of atrocity stories that, for some, propaganda implied "atrocity propaganda." On the Allied side there were many atrocity reports that could be neither proved nor disproved, but there were many more that were later officially admitted to be false.[19] There was, for example, a revolting and quite untrue story of the mutilation of a British nurse in Belgium that was circulated in the early days of the war. It was later proved that those responsible for its circulation knew that it was false from the very beginning and that it was nothing more than a conscious and deliberate lie.[20] But undoubtedly the most shocking of the atrocity stories invented by the Allies was that of the "Corpse Factory." In brief, it was simply a report that the Germans boiled down the corpses of their soldiers for fats, and it was founded on a deliberate mistranslation of the German word *Kadaver* which, although it means literally "a corpse," is used in German to refer only to the body of an animal and never to that of a man. The circulation of this story throughout the world was "encouraged and connived at by both the Government and the Press."[21] It was intended primarily to destroy any pro-German sympathies, especially in the Far East. Although it was first invented in 1917, it was not finally disposed of until 1925 when it was admitted in the House of Commons that it was false.

Atrocity propaganda is particularly dangerous as a form of propaganda in the tense atmosphere of a nation at war, for what begins as a minor fabrication can very easily become a monstrous perversion of the truth. In the first place, a belief in the truth of the appalling practices described by the propagandists must inevitably have the effect, in some cases, of inciting revenge in similar acts of cruelty. These in turn would call forth reprisals of an equally barbarous nature from the enemy.[22] The Allies, say, would invent an atrocity story about the Germans, which might incite the Allied troops to genuine acts of reprisal, which in turn would lead the Germans, now feeling themselves to be the aggrieved party, to take drastic revenge. When revealed, these retaliation atrocities would be used as evidence to prove the truth and justice of the original, invented story. The whole vicious circle of story inciting action and action inspiring story in time would become so involved that it would be impossible to determine original causes or the extent to which each was responsible for the other. There has, as yet, been little detailed research into this problem and apart from establishing that there is a definite causal relationship between atrocity stories and actual atrocities, little is really known of the extent of such a relationship.[23]

It is curious to note here that although in the First World War atrocity stories of an extremely gruesome character were staple propaganda fare for all belligerents, actual atrocities were much less common, whereas in the Second World War, although practices of almost unbelievable bestiality were committed on an unprecedented scale, relatively little attention was paid to atrocity propaganda. The one notable exception was the very special case of the films taken when the Allied armies reached the more notorious Nazi concentration camps. As atrocity propaganda these films were unusual in that their horror was less than the truth. Belsen could not be exaggerated. It was only along the Soviet front that both the Russians and the Germans gave to atrocity propaganda anything like the emphasis it was given by all the powers in 1914-1918.

SOME EFFECTS OF WAR PROPAGANDA ON THE POSTWAR WORLD

One reason given by Lasswell [24] for the increased interest in propaganda in the 1920's was what he described as a "new inquisitiveness" in the world. Another, and a more direct explanation, was that the "credulous utopianism" of the mass of the people, stemming mainly from the artificial optimism created by the wartime propagandists, had given way to cynicism and disenchantment. The world had not developed as its leaders had promised and the people, according to their temperament, were uneasy, puzzled, or angered at the unknown cunning that had apparently deceived and degraded them. The formulation of a positive program for the political and social reorganization of Europe, as proposed by Moysset at the Inter-Allied Propaganda Conference in 1918, may have given new heart to the Allies, but the people were soon brought to realize that their hopes for a better world were to be frustrated. They therefore wanted to know more about the workings of a propaganda that could so mislead them.

The success of war propaganda ensured its place in all future political maneuvers, a fact which Lasswell and others believed indicated the great menace of propaganda. An art which had been developed when nations were fighting for their existence was being turned into a science applicable to every political contest. Propaganda was, of course, a force in politics long before the war, but the war provided the opportunity for far-reaching experiments in new techniques. It also brought the occupation of propagandist into the limelight for the first time, and there is no doubt that the apparent power and influence of the propagandist led many power-seekers to emulate his methods. In this way, therefore, the propaganda of 1914-1918 stimulated an enormous increase in the volume of propaganda in peace-time political activity.

It was during the First World War, too, that many nations for the first time became efficiently-organized units. Through the use of propaganda, patriots became aware of their traditions, their customs, and then of their responsibilities. It will be recalled that one of the objectives of Allied policy was to encourage the national aspirations of the races dominated by the Austrian Empire. President Wilson, for example, proclaimed that an independent Czech-Slovak republic would follow victory by the Allies. To some extent, therefore, the propagandists helped to shape the new organization of Europe. National symbols and slogans acquired a new significance, for in the absence of a national tradition or history they were the only force capable of creating a sense of national identity. At the same time the whole idea of the nation as an entity became more concrete, more purposeful, and more meaningful.[25]

In addition, the propaganda that made it possible for people to see their government as a strong organization, tended to make these same people more submissive to authority and more receptive to non-rational propaganda appeals in general.

Another problem arose from the fact that most of the first accounts of war propaganda, whether in the form of memoirs by the propagandists or of exposures of their dishonest practices, tended to stress the novel, the spectacular and the sensational. This was to be expected, for naturally such tactics make more exciting reading than the routine and the prosaic. But it did influence the subsequent study of propaganda by adding weight to the idea that all propaganda is essentially something sensational or irrational, and thereby complicated its objective study.

Four

THE TECHNIQUES OF PROPAGANDA

The propagandist works on the minds of other men, seeking to influence their attitudes and thereby their actions. The measure of his success is the apparent willingness with which they do the things he wants them to do, whether it be to vote for his party, to accept with good grace a higher price for food, to make sacrifices now for victory later, or to take the pledge.

No matter what the object of his campaign, the propagandist will almost certainly come up against a certain amount of opposition. Indeed the only reason why the particular skills of the propagandist are called for is because such opposition exists. There is no need for propaganda to encourage people to do what they were determined to do anyway, although some propagandists have enormously enhanced their own prestige and the reputation of their profession for infallibility by making a great deal of noise and display at the rear of a popular movement which they afterwards claim to have inspired and led. The propagandist's aims may be frustrated and opposed by various obstacles. There is, first of all, the competition of rival propagandists that, as well as providing direct counter-propaganda, can in some circumstances so condition public opinion that no form of propaganda is able to produce automatic response. Again, propaganda can achieve only limited success against strongly entrenched attitudes or against basic human instincts. For instance it is easier to arouse hysterical hatred and fear of an enemy in time of war than to inculcate a spirit of universal brotherly love in time of peace. A third source of difficulty for the propagandist lies in the danger or the hardship of a proposed activity. This is met variously in campaigns ranging from the appeal to fight and perhaps to die for one's country, to the annual request to "Give to the Community Chest." Finally there is what might be called the "inertia of public opinion," what Mosca had described as the "conservatism" of the masses, which makes it so much easier to strengthen allegiance to an existing faith than to win converts to a new faith. Skilled party propagandists, who have long recognized this, concentrate on making sure that their own supporters turn out to vote and concern themselves less with winning over the opposition. Writing at the turn of the century, Ostrogorski described such popular election tactics as special parades, bands, noise and spectacle, "political" picnics, barbecues and dances, and the display of emblems, flags, and stickers with the comment (substantiated by modern research) that, while all these things won few new votes for the party, they roused enthusiasm and awakened the apathetic who were already aligned with the party.[1]

To get his message across, despite all obstacles, the propagandist needs a number of very special talents. He must first of all be a skilled psychologist with a deep understanding of the complexities of the human mind and its motivations. Throughout history certain men have had an intuitive grasp of psychological principles. But propaganda on a large, systematic scale had to wait until the development of modern experimental psychology gave rise to a science with a substantial body of data and a means of training people in its use.

The propagandist must address a particular group in a particular time and place. If he is to succeed in influencing that group, he must know how it is composed; he must be aware of the nature and strength of existing attitudes to the subject of his campaign; and he must also know enough history and sociology to understand how these attitudes came into being. The larger the group, the more complicated are the motives which guide it. When one reaches a group as large as the nation, one has to appeal to many sides of human nature even to the extent of being contradictory. It was, said Mosca, a general rule that:

> If a system of ideas, feelings, is to be accepted by great masses of human beings, it must address the loftier sentiments of the human spirit: it must promise that justice and equality will reign in this world, or in some other, or it must proclaim that the good will be rewarded and the wicked punished. At the same time it will not go far wrong if it yields some small satisfaction to the envy and rancor that are generally felt toward the powerful and the fortunate and intimates that, in this life, or in some other, there will come a time when the last shall be first and the first last. It will help if some phase of the doctrine can manage to offer a refuge for good souls, gentle souls, who seek in meditation and resignation some solace from the conflicts and disappointments of life. It will be useful, also—one might even say indispensable—for the doctrine to have some means of utilizing the spirit of abnegation and sacrifice that predominates in certain individuals and of guiding it into proper channels, though the same doctrine must also leave some little elbowroom for pride and vanity.[2]

One of the first stages in a propaganda campaign is to determine the rational or non-rational content of the message. A non-rational appeal allows even greater range of choice for it can be focused on a wide variety of emotions and instincts common to the whole human race—fear, self-preservation, aggressiveness, love, gregariousness, and so on—and it may also be directed at those racial characteristics, historical traditions and cultural features peculiar to any one nation at any one period of history.

Another common technique of propaganda is to transfer the emotional attitudes aroused by one situation over to another which may in itself have been incapable of arousing any significant response at all. That is to say, for example, a propagandist for the cause of Nordic superiority might use the record of Japanese barbarisms in the Pacific War to arouse the anger and hatred of his audience against those responsible for them. He might then attempt to transfer those emotional reactions to other Japanese living peaceful and inoffensive lives on the Pacific Coast of America. There might be no logical connection justifying any such transfer, but experience has shown that once an emotional attitude is aroused it will tend to embrace other situations introduced at the same time. The emotional transfer can also operate not only from person to person, but from person to thing and back again. The nation's flag can become a symbol of the nation's history and can evoke the pride and courage originally inspired by the record of great deeds. In turn, the respect for the flag can be transferred to the one who carries it, or to those responsible for its safekeeping. An awareness of the force of this kind of transfer and the ability to stimulate it is one of the major weapons in the propagandist's armory.[3]

The propagandist will not succeed unless he can make full mental contact with his audience, speaking a language they will understand and displaying some kind of emotional sympathy with their attitudes. The fanatical extremist does not usually make a good propagandist because of his failure to appreciate that others can, with equal sincerity and good will, hold opposing views. This is the weakness of much Communist propaganda originating in or inspired by Moscow. It is couched in the pedantic terminology of those who see in Marxism the culmination of political wisdom and in all other faiths nothing more than criminal folly. It is full of such phrases as "Capitalist lackeys," "Fascist hyenas," "bourgeois decadence" and the like, phrases which strike no responsive chord from the working class in the Western democracies.

The failure to communicate is something more than failure to use the correct local idiom. It involves the whole manner of presenting propaganda. The selection of such details as the color and texture of paper, the layout, the use and style of illustration, the type face, binding, and format in general must be guided by the customs of those for whom it is intended.[4]

So far this chapter has been concerned with the material content of the propaganda message, with such things as the text of a pamphlet, the script of a speech or film, the situation portrayed in a drawing or cartoon, the wording of a banner, or the symbolism of a flag or uniform. Discussions of propaganda material involve considerations of truth and falsehood, emotional or rational forms of expression, and questions of fact or opinion. Having once determined this material the propagandist must then see that it reaches his audience. The techniques of communication by which the propagandist transmits his material to an audience can be conveniently termed the "instruments of propaganda" and these can in turn be classified as "primary" and "secondary" instruments.

The primary instruments, which are the actual forms in which the propaganda material is presented, demonstrate the propagandist's amazing versatility and ingenuity. Propagandists have used for their primary instruments: speeches, rumors, telephone messages, rallies and demonstrations (including exhibitions of violence), marches, uniforms and costumes with badges, buttons and armbands, flags and banners, civil, military, and religious ceremonies, advertisements, billboards, posters and chalked slogans, architecture, postage stamps, fairs, exhibitions and circuses, plays and films, photographs, paintings and cartoons, books, newspapers, pamphlets, circulars, broadsheets, leaflets, stickers, and every other form of the written word, fireworks and sky-writing, economic assistance programs, and indeed every conceivable means of communication between man and man.

The secondary instruments are the channels of communications, or means of distribution, by which the propagandist carries his material as embodied in the primary instruments to a distant or more extensive audience. They consist principally of newspaper presses, radio stations, postal and telegraph systems, roads and railways, theaters, education systems, publishing houses, and every kind of political, social or religious organization.

There are definite stages in planning the dissemination of propaganda. Having determined his objectives, the propagandist must decide on the material most likely to arouse the appropriate attitudes. At this stage he has to choose not only the general content of his message, but also the literary or artistic form in which it will be presented. This form may range from the calmly reasoned to the frankly scurrilous.

The propagandist's next consideration is the selection of the most suitable primary instruments to carry the message to the audience. Here he must consider the four basic criteria of successful propaganda—it must be seen, understood, remembered and acted upon.[5] He must make sure that not only is his propaganda accessible to his audience, but that they do in fact see it against a background of competing influences, that having seen it they will take from it the impression the propagandist intended to convey, and that the impression will remain with them long enough for them to act upon it. This means that the propagandist must take into account the size and the broad intellectual level of his audience, the existing attitudes of the audience to both the situation envisaged by the propagandist and to the propagandist himself, the extent to which the audience has access to the various media of communication, and the presence of competing propaganda or other non-propaganda influences.

That is to say, taking the size and intellectual level of the audience first, a street-corner meeting, appropriate enough in elections at ward level, would not be the best way to reach the nation's housewives, any more than a newspaper would be a practical means of reaching an illiterate peasant population. Normally, a government propagandist, with the entire resources of the state at his disposal, will adopt several techniques, each adding to and strengthening the others. The radio might be used first to get the material to as many people as quickly as possible, giving it that sense of urgency which a radio message can convey. The newspaper would follow more slowly, confirming and amplifying the original statement and at the same time presenting it in a more durable form. Once interest is aroused in this way, the work of influencing attitudes might then be further consolidated by a series of public meetings and workers' discussion groups explaining the importance of the earlier announcements.

The existing attitude of the audience to the propagandist and his message must also be considered. Open Russian propaganda to the United States, for example, suffers the disadvantage that most of it is rejected simply because of its Russian origin. The Russian propagandist knows that the first reaction to his every proposal and suggestion will be to dismiss it as a "Communist propaganda stunt."

The availability of primary instruments of communication to the audience seriously modifies the type of campaign that can be conducted. The United States has the technical ability to launch an intensive radio propaganda campaign against Communist China, but in a country where only three in every thousand possess a receiving set, the time and effort would be largely wasted. In countries such as India, Egypt, or Turkey where, until very recently at least, there was something over 90 per cent female illiteracy, propaganda addressed to the women through newspapers or leaflets would make no impact at all. In the United States over 90 per cent of the college-educated read one or more of the nearly 8,000 periodicals published regularly; but only some 50 per cent of those with less than a high school education read any magazines at all. Also, within the United States, newspaper circulation per thousand of population ranges from a high of just over 1,000 in the District of Columbia to a low of slightly over 100 in Mississippi. In Pakistan, India, Burma, and Haiti, there are less than 10 newspapers sold for each 1,000 of population. The propagandist must be fully alive to such statistics as far as they affect any area of people he deals with and he must adjust his means of propaganda accordingly.

The presence of competing propaganda has also to be taken into account in selecting the primary instruments of communication. The nature of competing propaganda probably has an even greater effect on the selection and styling of material. The chief concern of the propagandist in these circumstances is to avoid exposing himself to counter-propaganda by a rival who possesses vastly superior resources in any particular means of communication. Competition also comes from many non-political sources: the billboard urging us to "Vote Smith for Progress and Prosperity" may seem a powerful piece of work in the campaign office, but it may not even be noticed amidst twenty others crying the virtues of soaps, motels, gasoline, and beer; the politician speaking on a nationwide network may go unheard if the local station is broadcasting the "Top Tunes of Today." Within dictatorships it is possible to avoid competition more easily than in a democracy. Hitler, for example, had no fear that the German people might prefer another program when he wished to speak to them. There was no other program.

> When Hitler speaks the people of Germany must listen wherever they are. Factory sirens blow, there is a minute or two of silence, and then the voice bursts forth. Loudspeakers in public places relay the speech; not to listen, or appear to listen, is disloyalty. The penetration of politicised radio into the entire national consciousness is then complete, its power inescapable.[6]

The selection of the primary instruments of propaganda is governed by one further factor, the availability of the secondary instruments: the printing presses, the radio stations, the paper supplies, the meeting halls, and so on, possession of which controls the planning of any propaganda campaign. The legal right to disseminate ideas through the primary instruments of propaganda, a "free press" or "freedom of assembly," has little real value unless there is also reasonable access to the secondary instruments. As Bertrand Russell once pointed out,[7] there is no equality of propaganda in a society where the press, radio stations and film studios are available to only one economic class. The 1936 Constitution of the Soviet Union guarantees freedom of speech, of the press, of assembly and mass meeting, and of street processions and demonstrations, but it then restricts the effect of this guarantee "by placing at the disposal of the toilers and their organizations printing presses, stocks of paper, public buildings, the streets, means of communication and other material requisites for the exercise of these rights." [8] Free speech is a privilege of the Communist party and those organizations in which the Communist party provides the leadership.

Apart from the principles which apply to propaganda in general, there are a number of problems peculiar to each of the various media of communication that can be considered here under a few broad headings.

PROPAGANDA THROUGH
THE SPOKEN WORD

Certain individuals such as Pericles, the Athenian, or Daniel O'Connell, the Irish patriot, have appeared in every age, with the power to speak their way into the minds and hearts of men and so to influence the course of events. That the human voice is still an undiminished force in politics is evidenced by the speed with which Hitler's fanatic polemics drove his people to war and destruction and by the extent to which the courage of the British people in 1940-41 was sustained by the oratory of Churchill. With the advent of broadcasting there has been a profound change in the character of public speaking which has affected both the manner of presentation and its effect upon the audience.

The radio speaker can reach an audience of millions, instead of hundreds or perhaps thousands, but this increased range is bought at the price of personal contact. The broadcaster who cannot be sure he is in rapport with his listeners is unable to adjust his material or style to their changing moods; and while he remains unaware of the effect of his words, he is unable to draw support from audience reaction.

Trying to get the best of both worlds by broadcasting a speech at a public meeting solves only part of the problem because the home audience, lacking the emotional impact of being members of a crowd, are likely to react to crowd appeals in unexpected and unsuspected ways. Of course the disadvantages are not all with the broadcaster. He is at least free from the interruption of hecklers. He is not embarrassed, nor are his listeners disturbed, by those who walk out of his meeting. The broadcaster is not nearly so concerned about holding the attention of every member of his audience, for those who continue to listen are unaware of those who switch off. And, because the broadcaster is unaffected by the reactions of his audience, his speech is likely to be read from a carefully prepared and rehearsed script. The qualities of the radio speaker tend to become those of the professional actor, rather than those of the extempore orator.

The effect of broadcasting can also be seen in the declining importance of the non-broadcast speech. Surveys of modern elections have shown that party meetings in the village hall have little impact on voting behavior. The few who still attend them are the truly dedicated members of the party sponsoring the speaker, with a small sprinkling of equally dedicated members of the opposition. Meetings of this kind are part of the ritual of electioneering, and they continue to be held more out of habit and the desire to preserve the ritual than for any positive contribution they make to the party's victory. Much the same sort of comment can be made of the "whistle-stop" tours of the great names in the party's hierarchy. Here, however, one must be careful to distinguish between the votes which might be won by addressing two hundred people at a country railroad station (an insignificant matter which would not justify the time and expense involved) and the votes which might be won by reporting to an audience of several million that the great man was sufficiently interested in the ordinary people to take time to address two hundred of them at a time.

In two respects radio broadcasting demonstrates its supremacy over all other media of communication. It is immediate and it is universal, being bounded by neither time nor space. It is immediate in the sense that there is no time lag between the speaking and the hearing of the message. A broadcast address by the President of the United States to Congress would be heard by listeners in London and Rome before some of those actually watching the President speak.

Broadcasting is universal because it cannot easily be stopped at national frontiers. "Jamming" is at best an uncertain device, while the resort to "jamming" is in itself an admission of weakness. Even in so rigid a dictatorship as that of Nazi Germany, it was found impossible to prevent people listening regularly to Allied news broadcasts. At one stage in 1944, the BBC was broadcasting nearly 230 news bulletins a day beamed to every part of the world in forty-eight different languages.[9] The United States was slower in entering into international broadcasting propaganda campaigns, but by 1950 the *Voice of America,* which is under the control of a division of the State Department, was broadcasting daily in twenty-four languages.[10]

At one time it was imagined that the international character of radio would make it an instrument of universal peace and good will. In 1935, for example, two psychologists wrote that "Any device that carries messages instantaneously and inexpensively to the farthest and most inaccessible regions of the earth, that penetrates all manner of social, political, and economic barriers, is by nature a powerful agent of democracy." [11] Despite the extensive use of radio as an international propaganda medium by the Soviet Union and the speed with which the Nazis made use of the unique political potentialities of radio to impress the power and permanence of their regime upon the German people, this naïvely optimistic view persisted probably until 1939, after which time such idealism died. Radio is now accepted by all the major states as a legitimate instrument of power politics. It has become "the most powerful single instrument of political warfare the world has ever known. More flexible in use and infinitely stronger in emotional impact than the printed word, as a weapon of *war waged psychologically* radio has no equal." [12]

Apart from its unique characteristics of immediacy and universality radio has now the added advantage that it is the most popular means of mass communication ever known. Statistics on the distribution of radio and television receivers in all industrially-advanced countries make it obvious that broadcasting is potentially an exceptionally powerful media for mass opinion control. This is not to say that it has yet realized this potential for there are, of course, a number of inhibiting factors. In the United States, for example, radio rose to eminence, and remains, primarily as entertainment. Political commentary and attempts to mold political attitudes must compete with music, soap operas, comedy and sports programs and, if listener-research figures are to be believed, the political broadcaster comes out second best except on infrequent and special occasions. The organization of American broadcasting into four major networks, with a very large number of independent stations, all financially independent of the government, makes its domination by the government or by one political party extremely unlikely, although even now it is able to exclude effectively certain minor or currently unpopular political groupings.

Listener-research figures also indicate wide variations in listening habits.[13] Generally the amount of radio listening increases with education and economic status although those with higher income and education tend to become more discriminating listeners, deliberately selecting particular programs rather than leaving the radio "on" simply as background noise. Other surveys indicate that while the sex difference in listening habits is marked in Moslem countries, it is of little significance in the United States, and that urban people generally listen more regularly than rural people.

Much has been said and written about the impact of radio upon public opinion and the extent to which it is subject to deliberate manipulation. For obvious reasons, these effects are not susceptible to precise analysis. Nevertheless, certain generalizations can be made that indicate the areas in which radio appears to have had the greatest social influence.[14]

In the first place the speed and range of radio communication has generally speeded up the whole process of the formation and exchange of ideas. Political ideologies which once took a generation to spread over a land may be disseminated, accepted with enthusiasm, and then rejected within the space of a few years. One of the consequences of this may be a more rapid turnover of the fortunes of the political parties, and a quicker rise and fall of political demagogues.

Radio has a personal and dramatic influence far in excess of the appeal of the printed word. The full impact of radio drama was never more fearfully illustrated than when, in October, 1938, the Orson Welles broadcast of *The War of the Worlds* created mass hysteria and something approaching national panic. Offsetting the dramatic impact of radio, however, is its ephemeral character. The effect of radio is immediate, but transitory, and, once the broadcast is over, the effect is gone. The listener has no permanent record of what has been said, and if he wishes confirmation of some point he must wait until it appears in print. Unlike the reader who, if his attention is distracted, can set his book aside or go back over a passage, the listener is tied to the pace of the broadcast so that what he misses is lost forever.

Radio propaganda can have a considerable effect on the political maturity of the electorate in that it can inspire a greater interest in political affairs. Radio has enabled more people, particularly those in remote areas, to participate directly in current political controversies and perhaps even to take a greater share in direct political action. Such things as direct broadcasts from legislative assemblies, party conventions, and political rallies can give people a more direct contact with political life than could possibly be gathered simply from press reports. This of course implies that the radio provides a forum for political controversy and that the controversy which is broadcast is genuine disagreement on matters of some current significance. A broadcasting system in a democracy which confines its "controversial" programs to academic wranglings over issues long dead or to inconsequential trivia fails to give the service it is technically equipped to provide.

It is one of the paradoxes of radio that while it can and does stimulate wider public discussion it is also the most powerful agency yet discovered for inducing conformity and unity. The audience of radio is essentially a mass audience. Its standards are the standards of the mass which means that in the authoritarian regime, where radio is a government monopoly, its propaganda is concentrated on such simple mass emotional appeals as xenophobia; whereas when radio becomes primarily a commercial enterprise, as in the United States, its standards are the lowest common denominator of public taste. In either situation, radio attempts to appeal to the greatest possible audience at the expense of minority groups or of ideas of limited circulation. Radio has brought the fulfillment of J. S. Mill's prophecy of the trends of democracy:

> Comparatively speaking they now read the same things, see the same things, go to the same places, have their hopes and fears directed to the same objects, have the same rights and liberties, and the same means of asserting them.[15]

This trend to conformity also manifests itself in the increasing importance of national politics as against local issues, a trend which has, of course, been accelerated by broadcasting. Radio has brought national political figures into a prominence in small communities which would have been unthinkable in days of more primitive communication. As people have become increasingly aware of the problems of government "at the center" and have been able to follow the development of these problems as they have occurred, they have become more conscious of the "larger issues at stake." Local politics, in consequence, have been relegated to a comparatively minor role.

Television introduces several further problems for the propagandist. The first of these is that the television viewer must pay more attention to the program than need the radio listener. Most of us are familiar with the ease with which the modern student is able to read and write against the background of radio music, but most of those who have attempted to combine studying with viewing will admit that television is a more demanding distraction. While it commands the attention of the viewer, however, television makes fewer demands upon his mind and imagination. Something that can be seen and heard is clearly much easier to follow and understand than something which can merely be heard. Television is thus an unusually potent instrument

of public-opinion control. It first captures its audience and
then relaxes it to the extent, in extreme cases, of complete
intellectual lethargy. Its appeal is intimate, personal and
dramatic. A television show is, however, extremely costly
to produce, which means that those responsible for it exert
themselves to make it as near perfect as possible, in the
technical sense at least. The social impact of television has
been very neatly summed up by Albig:

> In television the association of current symbolic personal-
> ities with the groups, abstractions and values which they
> have come to represent is more standardized than has
> been true of communication by word, picture or radio.
> Excessive identification of abstractions, groups and values
> with particular individuals who become symbols is always
> the too-ready response of large publics untutored in ra-
> tional analysis of public issues. Trivial, oversimplified and
> vulgarly personalized impressions result. This is a strength
> of democratic decision making, in that it keeps the social
> process humanized and partially corrects or cancels the
> inhuman abstractions to which all specialists are prone.
> But personification also corrodes or inhibits more rational
> and analytical reflection on public issues. Television diffuses
> and standardizes personal images as no other agency has
> done. A televised cabinet meeting is not, and, for political
> reasons, could not be, a real working cabinet meeting.
> Therefore, the public is not watching responsible govern-
> ment in action, but a political show of humanized states-
> men at play, though ostensibly at work. Is this in the
> public interest? [16]

While radio still dominates in the sphere of international
communication, its role in internal affairs has been taken
over by television in the technically advanced countries.
This is not to say that domestic radio is declining. Indeed,
statistics show that even in such a television-oriented country
as the United States, the number of radio sets in use contin-
ues to rise year by year. But radio broadcasting has changed
in character. In many homes there are several radios, including portable transistor sets, but these are intended
primarily to provide a local news service and a background
of popular music for other activities. Television has come
to be the chief source of commentaries, films, documen-
taries, plays and other programs that might influence
opinions.

Despite a great mass of literature about the social significance of radio and television, our knowledge of the actual effect of these media on public behavior is limited. While generalizations of the enormous social impact of sight and sound broadcasting on our social and economic life are commonplace, and probably for the most part valid, they should still be treated with some reserve. It would perhaps be safer to regard all observations of this kind as reasoned probabilities rather than as authoritative conclusions.

There are other forms of spoken-word propaganda, most of them, however, operating on a relatively small scale and over a short period of time. Perhaps the most important is the deliberate circulation of rumors, particularly those that spread slander and gossip about some candidate for office. This can be an exceptionally vicious form of propaganda made doubly unattractive by the fact that those responsible for the rumors usually manage to remain undetected, if not unsuspected. Rumors have, however, the disadvantage that, once put into circulation, they are uncontrollable. A rumor that becomes distorted, as most rumors quickly become, may have effects quite contrary to those originally intended.

Rumors circulate most rapidly and are listened to most attentively in an atmosphere of crisis or emergency, or when important events are taking place but where those concerned have no clear picture of what is happening. Rumors circulate widely during air raids, floods, riots, among crowds waiting for some event, in prisons, among the spectators at accidents and fires; in short in all sorts of events where the situation is tense, but where official news is lacking.[17] One of the functions of the German "Fifth Column" agents in France in 1940 was to spread rumors which would disrupt morale and create panic. In the absence of up-to-date authoritative news, the rumors largely succeeded in their purpose. The disorder and confusion they caused then stimulated the spontaneous circulation of other rumors which further intensified the disorder and confusion. A number of experiments[18] have shown that, once a rumor gains some credence in a time of intense emotional stress, there will be many who will continue to believe in it and to reject official denials issued in a calmer atmosphere.

There are several other ways in which spoken propaganda can be disseminated: through telephones, public address systems, loudspeaker vans, phonograph records and so on; but none of these introduce any major problems not covered by what has already been written here. There is, therefore, no need to describe them in detail.

WRITTEN PROPAGANDA

The written expression of ideas can be communicated in so many ways that a detailed review of all possible forms of written propaganda would be a practical impossibility. Apart from the more orthodox media, propagandists, in their more fanciful moments, have resorted to innumerable "novelty" tactics ranging from sky-writing to stone-cutting. The U. S. Republican party in 1956 marketed a special brand of *I Like Ike* cigarettes, while in 1950, in Great Britain, the sugar concern of Tate and Lyle Ltd. appealed directly to the consumer with anti-nationalization slogans printed on every packet of sugar. Such devices may be extremely effective in a short-term campaign, but most propaganda is still conveyed through the larger media and attention will therefore be concentrated on books and newspapers.

Books have always been one of the commoner means for disseminating propaganda, but generally their appeal is to small and usually specialized publics. Books have little immediate impact on public opinion simply because very few people read books. Even in a country such as the United States where illiteracy has been reduced to insignificant proportions, book reading is not a widely developed habit. A recent survey showed that 48 per cent of the adult population of America had read no books at all in the preceding year and an additional 25 per cent had read fewer than ten books. Some 10 per cent of the adult population accounted for two-thirds of all book reading done during the year.[19]

It does not always follow, however, that because a book is not widely read that it has no influence at all on public opinion. Often the general theme of some particularly controversial book may become widely known by comment, review, and digest through the more popular media of communication. There is always, of course, the danger that the version which reaches the public in this way will be a garbled misinterpretation of the original, but it will be these "popular" versions that will guide public opinion. The fact that very few people have read Darwin's *Origin of the Species* has not stopped large numbers from entering into passionate and bitter debate over his evolutionary theories—usually attributing to him statements and opinions nowhere to be found in his writings. The political significance of a book is likely to arise less from what it says than from what it is commonly believed to say.

Compared with other instruments of propaganda books suffer the further disadvantage that they are relatively expensive and difficult to acquire. The book does not force itself upon the attention of the reader. Unlike the radio it does not intrude into the privacy of the home, nor is it delivered with the newspaper. The would-be reader has to make a conscious effort to visit a library or bookshop, or in small communities, where there are no bookshops and the libraries are inadequate, he must order by mail. This means that the book buyer tends to be more aware of what he wants and therefore to be less affected by spur-of-the-moment decisions. The propaganda the book reader receives is for this reason more likely to be that of his own choosing. Another difficulty with books arises from their proliferation. So many new titles are produced each year[20] that any one book tends to be lost in the mass of material available. Even the most voracious readers find it quite impossible to keep up with all the new material published, although they might confine themselves to one particular field. The propagandist who tries to reach the book-reading public must therefore follow this trend and repeat his ideas under several titles in the hope that most of those he wishes to influence will read at least one of them.

The propaganda contained in a book may be either direct or indirect. The propaganda is direct if the whole book is devoted to some particular political theme, the treatment of which may range from the profound academic study to the hysterical diatribe. Most books which attempt to evaluate such things as democracy, socialism, fascism, the New Deal, segregation, or colonial independence fall into this category. Indirect propaganda is found in books in which the author makes incidental pronouncements or assumptions of political significance. There are, for example, a large number of detective stories wherein the efforts of the hero to solve the mystery are hampered by a bureaucracy, civil servants and police, which are inefficient, strangling in their own red tape, or even corrupt. Some authors invariably make their villain an East European or an Asiatic. It is, however, rather dangerous and misleading to attempt to assess the volume of propaganda in fiction by cataloguing all such prejudiced assumptions and inferences. The essential feature of propaganda is that it be deliberate and therefore, before an author could be accused of propaganda, it would be necessary to show that he consciously selected his stereotypes for civil servants, Italians, domestic servants or capitalists.

Although many factors, some of which have been outlined here, reduce the value of books as propaganda, books have a number of special advantages which will ensure their continued use in the attempt to mold and persuade public opinion. The first of these is the prestige that attaches to books. There is a widespread feeling that because an opinion is printed between hard covers it acquires an authority that it would not otherwise have. Also, books have a permanent value. The newspaper is read and then discarded, but the book is preserved and perhaps read again. The fact that it is preserved also means that the reader can refer to it whenever he chooses. This in turn suggests that the book is likely to make a deeper impression than the newspaper or the radio because the reader normally selects a book when his general state of mind is most receptive to the ideas contained in it. Again, a book is considerably longer than the fullest newspaper report and it can therefore develop its argument more fully, anticipating and answering a great many of the counter-arguments. It can give added emphasis to an opinion by repetition and rephrasing.

In general, the book is unsatisfactory in a short-term propaganda campaign. It takes too long to produce and to market while its effect is felt only slowly. But if the intention is to create deep and lasting attitudes the book is an essential addition to any other propaganda media. Its value lies in its permanence and prestige that enable it to reinforce, confirm and consolidate ideas that were first given a wider hearing through more "popular" channels.

Newspapers are perhaps the most pervasive carriers of news and opinion. They are cheap, readily available, and, apart from the Sunday editions of some American papers, they do not take long to read. The prime service of the daily newspaper is usually stated as the giving of information about, and the interpretation of, public affairs. The term "public affairs" is loosely applied to events ranging from local crime to international war. Surveys have shown us,[21] however, that the newspaper serves several other functions which, to many readers, are far more important than its news content. Such informational services as television and theater programs, shipping notices, stock exchange reports, and super-market advertisements have become valuable aids to everyday life. The "comics," and magazine features, are read for entertainment. The newspaper's personal columns, social notes, birth, death, and marriage notices, and human interest stories provide some readers with a highly valued form of social contact.

One of the most obvious implications of these varied motives for reading newspapers is that a paper's circulation is not necessarily a measure of its political influence. It is not unknown, for example, for large numbers of people to subscribe to a newspaper whose politics they reject, and whose political commentaries they never read, but which provides an unusually thorough coverage of all sporting events. Many politically-oriented newspapers recognize this and deliberately try to build up circulation through popular features in the hope that at least a few new readers will be attracted to, and perhaps influenced by, its political commentaries.

One of the greatest advantages of the newspaper as a propaganda medium is that it is possible to direct appeals to different reading publics in the style and language most likely to appeal to that public. This is particularly noticeable in a dictatorship where one authority determines the policy to be followed by all newspapers, even though it might allow considerable editorial discretion in the manner in which that policy is interpreted for the readers. In Nazi Germany, for example, the once highly respected *Frankfurter Zeitung* and the party paper *Der Angriff* both gave unqualified support to the Nazi regime although their journalistic styles were as far apart as those of *The Times* and the *Daily News* in New York. Even within the democracies, the propagandist for any one party or pressure group has to recognize that each newspaper has its own relatively distinct reading public, that most readers rarely see a newspaper other than the ones to which they regularly subscribe, and that if his propaganda is to have its maximum effect, it must be adapted to the journalistic tastes of a particular group of readers. Journalistic treatment varies not only between papers, but often from section to section of the one paper. The clichés of the editorials are generally more ponderous and moralistic than those of the foreign news page, while domestic news is written in a manner quite distinct from that of the financial columns. The popular newspaper has developed a vocabulary and literary style distinctively its own, designed to arouse the appropriate reaction. The cliché thus becomes, not a mark of laziness or ignorance, but an essential tool in newspaper communication. Carefully selected, it will almost automatically elicit the desired response from the casual reader. It has, of course, a greater influence on the large proportion of readers who do no more than skim the headlines and the main points of a story. The constant repetition of the same phrases to cover certain situations or to convey certain impressions saves the reader the effort of thought and interpretation. When he reads that "reformers are trying to bring order out of chaos," or that "so-called reformers would sacrifice the solid achievements of the past," he is likely to react to these familiar phrases in familiar ways. His attitude to the new situation will tend to be governed by his attitude to the situations to which they have been applied in the past.

Any doubts that even the news columns have propaganda significance can be settled by comparing the way in which several papers react to the one story. Each paper will make its own decision on the importance of the story—a decision which will be reflected in the page on which the story appears, its position on that page, and the size and style of type used in the headlines. Devices such as special type, illustrations or unusual layout may all serve to attract the readers' attention. Other factors include the length of the story, the manner in which it is rewritten and the extent to which its importance is emphasized by editorial comment and background feature articles. A report of new developments in, say, the Berlin situation, reported briefly but factually on page five of one paper, will make a very different impression if rewritten and featured on page one with the blackest of banner headlines, commented on in the first leader, and supported by a human-interest story on life in Berlin today.

At one time it was customary to distinguish the expression of opinion on the editorial pages of a paper from the straightforward presentation of facts on the news pages. With the growing appreciation of the extent to which opinion governs the selection and manner of presentation of news, it has been concluded that this division is unrealistic and it is now generally admitted that the news columns can also contain propaganda. This is especially true of news magazines such as *Time* and *Newsweek* where the selection and presentation of news items is an expression of editorial policy. But while this blending of news story and editorial comment is common, another surprising feature of the American press is the frequency with which editorial policy seems to be at odds with the selection of news. This was particularly noticeable during the period of the New Deal, when a great many papers that consistently attacked editorially the policies of President Roosevelt were prepared to report the successes and popular achievements of the New Deal on their news pages.

Other forms of press propaganda are the paid advertisements on political themes by organizations such as the American Independent Electric Light and Power Companies or the Committee for Constitutional Government; and the free copy supplied to newspapers by the public relations offices of the various interested groups in the community.[22] Another form is the cartoon which by selection, simplification, and the use of familiar symbols such as the GOP Elephant, John Q. Public, Colonel Blimp, *etc.*, is able to reduce a complex situation to a single emotional reaction. For this reason, the cartoon is one of the commonest and (in skilled hands) most effective forms of printed propaganda. It is the almost universal practice of modern newspapers to publish at least one political cartoon in every issue, and some cartoonists such as Low in England or Herblock in the United States have a tremendous reputation and influence, their cartoons being frequently reproduced in other papers even in other parts of the world. The comic strips, the Letters to the Editor, and the feature articles are additional sources of newspaper propaganda, especially for pressure groups and individuals who can in this way appeal to a wider public.

The press is the cheapest form of printed propaganda and in the long run the most important. Despite the enormous advances of radio and television, the newspaper is still the major source of political news and commentary in all civilized countries. The newspaper makes up for its lack of immediacy, compared to radio, by its durability and a largely self-created reputation of being the traditional crusader for the liberties of the people against the tyranny of Government. Further, the radio is thought of primarily as a form of entertainment, so that the news and comment that fill the bulk of the newspaper's columns (apart from the advertisements) are given a relatively minor place in radio programming. It is therefore unlikely, as long as there is a high percentage of literacy, that the newspaper will be replaced as the most important instrument for the communication of propaganda.

Although pamphlets are produced today in greater profusion than ever before, the great age of pamphleteering is over. Pamphlets are essentially protests about something; they thrive upon oppression and flourish best when they are illegal. A free press is the death of pamphleteers because it removes the first reason for the pamphlet's existence. The enormous circulation figures of modern pamphlets are a very misleading guide to their influence. The great bulk of them are given away free at meetings or are posted to legislators, civic leaders, editors, teachers, and so on, who are overwhelmed with printed paper and consign most of it to the wastepaper basket unread. Other pamphlets are sold to party enthusiasts, ostensibly to provide them with information, but really to supplement party funds.

Another great difficulty with pamphlets follows from their profusion. No bookshop could ever stock all the pamphlets produced, so most will refuse to stock any. This means that it is often extremely difficult to obtain copies of any one particular pamphlet, although one might be sent a hundred that are not wanted. The new media of mass communication, spoken and written, have replaced the pamphlet as a major instrument of propaganda. At best, it is a supplement to other propaganda tactics and a traditional element in the democratic election campaign where its absence would be noticed, but where its positive effect is probably insignificant.

MOTION PICTURES

One of the most famous producers of documentary films, John Grierson, once wrote of the motion picture in general that the propagandist had reason to be especially interested in it. The motion picture, he said, gives:

> . . . generous access to the public. It is capable of direct description, simple analysis and commanding conclusion, and may, by its tempo'd and imagistic powers, be made easily persuasive. It lends itself to rhetoric, for no form of description can add nobility to a simple observation so readily as a camera set low, or a sequence cut to a time-beat. But principally there is this thought that a single say-so can be repeated a thousand times a night to a million eyes, and, over the years, if it is good enough to live, to millions of eyes. That seven-leagued fact opens a new perspective, a new hope, to public persuasion.[29]

Grierson had grasped the reasons for the appeal of the motion picture, for its enormous influence on social and moral habits. He and others like him understood the psychological impact of the darkened cinema contrasted with the dramatic action, camera angles, close-ups, distortions and other technical tricks of film production on the screen.

Of all the mass communication media the motion picture is unexcelled in its ability to play upon the emotions of its audience, to penetrate and influence their needs, frustrations, ambitions and desires. Its appeal is essentially emotional so that, the more extensive and skillful its use of suggestion and subtle psychological conditioning, the more influential it is likely to be. It is no doubt true that many of the social practices influenced by films, i.e., styles of dress, mannerisms in speech, fads in decoration, habits of eating and drinking, etc., may be trivial, but the total effect of a large number of relatively unimportant appeals can be of serious social significance. Here it is interesting to note that the influence of motion pictures on social habits is both conservative and disruptive. In the realms of morals, of sex relations, and of such trivia as outlined above, the films have a liberalizing effect, rapidly breaking down old ideas and standards; but, in matters of nationalism, patriotism, religion, race, property rights, and social status, the effect of the motion picture has been generally to reinforce existing attitudes and to discourage any departure from the norm.[24]

One of the most striking means by which the cinema has influenced social attitudes has been through stereotypes—conventional figures that have come to be regarded as representative of particular occupations, races, or classes. In many instances the stereotype is so firmly established that individuals who depart from this artificial standard are either ignored or treated as unfortunate aberrations. To Hollywood all New York police are Irishmen; Prussian army officers all look like Conrad Veidt or Erich von Stroheim; the American Negro is depicted as a naïve, superstitious, lighthearted person who meets his problems by "shouting his way to glory"; Italians, "by some anthropological curse, are limited to restauranting or crime";[25] American children love their mothers, but have little respect for their fathers, unless the father is a doctor or a judge. The importance of stereotypes is increased by the opportunities afforded by the cinema for vicarious experience. The members of the audience not only see the portrayal of conventional roles, but in many cases actually identify themselves with the various characterizations. Spencer Tracy, as the "grown-up Eagle Scout, the Bumbling, Practical, Hard-headed but Soft-hearted AMERICAN," [26] is more than a cinema idol; his screen life is a model copied, more or less successfully, by thousands of American males. It is no doubt possible for the cinema to make more conscious and effective use of stereotypes than it has so far done. By the careful selection of appropriate stereotypes, the motion picture producers could go a long way toward directing large sections of public opinion to specific attitudes to such things as military discipline, national pride, racialism, radicals, foreigners, and "eggheads." There are, however, a number of reasons why the cinema, in democratic countries at least, is not as intensively used for propaganda as it could be.

From the very beginning, the production of British and American motion pictures had been thought of primarily as a competitive industry in which the goal is the highest possible profit and the means, the provision of entertainment. Although the cinema has had a significant influence on manners and morals, few of the big producers of feature films have concerned themselves directly with propaganda or education. Most have, in fact, rejected the imputation that they are guided by any other than the highest of motives, that of making money. The President of the British Board of Film Censors (an organization set up by the Trade itself), Lord Tyrrell, was happy to announce in 1936 that he had not so far licensed any film dealing with "current, burning political questions" and that he was prepared to put "some check" on those subjects which showed an interest in such topics. Cinema, he said, needed the "continued repression of controversy." [27] Even when, in the late 1930's, Hollywood made a number of films of the type of *Lives of a Bengal Lancer* and *Gunga Din,* the inspiration was more the commercial potentialities of the Empire market than the desire to extol the virtues of British Imperialism.

It costs a great deal of money to produce a motion picture. In the United States the cost of an average feature film is about one million dollars. Some exceptionally lavish productions have cost more than five million dollars and only the cheapest "B Grade" supporting films could be made for less than a quarter of a million.

> It is worth while to emphasize the fact that *one* motion picture costs twice as much to produce as it takes to purchase a large radio station, lock stock and barrel, and that the output of any studio in Hollywood for a period of three or four months involves enough capital to purchase a metropolitan newspaper.[28]

This fact of the high cost of film production, when taken with the fact of the profit motive, materially affects the use of motion pictures for propaganda. The economic structure of the film industry, in countries where it is a self-supporting industry, demands that its products be directed to the largest possible mass audience. A few films, mainly from small European studios, are designed for an intellectual-artistic minority, but the production of feature films generally is conditioned by the need to attract and hold an audience of millions. For this reason the standards of the motion picture are those of the mass. The plot and the manner of its treatment must be acceptable to the largest and least discriminating public. The producers, who wish to cover their investment, naturally tend to play safe, to repeat the uncomplicated stories of love, adventure, crime, and music that paid dividends before and to avoid offending the racial, religious, or national susceptibilities of groups large enough to affect seriously the box-office returns. Such propaganda as is contained in the general run of American, and British, motion pictures therefore tends to be "non-controversial," to confirm the accepted attitudes, especially those that reflect satisfaction with things as they are, and to set the seal of moral approval on the most popular aspirations. A few films, such as, for example, *Grapes of Wrath* or *The Ox-Bow Incident,* have raised doubts as to the validity of some cinema conventions, but such films represent only a very small fraction of the total number released.

The content of motion pictures is further conditioned by the fact that the producer is financially dependent upon an overseas market. The United States film industry receives anything from 25 per cent to 40 per cent of its gross income from abroad and in many cases it relies on the home market to cover costs and the foreign market to provide the profit. This means of course that the producer must be careful not to alienate too large a proportion of his foreign customers even in films intended primarily for the domestic market. The need to sell on a foreign market is a further obstacle to the production of "controversial" motion pictures, largely because most governments restrict the funds available to importers. The effect of currency limitations, in whatever form they are applied, is to restrict such pictures as can be imported to the safest commercial successes. With foreign films in any country this means invariably musicals, historical "costume" dramas, action films (adventure, crime and so on), and rowdy comedies, where dubbing into another language or subtitling cause the least inconvenience.

It is doubtful if there are any countries which do not apply some form of film censorship, whether it be undertaken by the state, the trade itself, private organizations, or any combination of these. Censorship regulations do not vary widely from country to country in regard to the type of material that should be banned. That is to say, almost all countries forbid material offensive to public morals, or likely to incite political or social unrest; but there is a wide divergence in the interpretation and application of these standards. The iron curtain countries, and dictatorships in general, are particularly sensitive to political controversy and can find sinister political implications in the most innocent and unexpected situations. In 1938 the Polish Government banned the American musical *Show Boat* because it considered the song "Ol' Man River" to be "proletarian propaganda" likely to incite the Polish masses to rebellion.

It would appear that, while the motion picture, considered purely in psychological terms, could be a most powerful medium for group persuasion, the economic structure of the film production industry in all countries where it is not a direct government enterprise reduces the political significance of the film to a relatively minor level, except perhaps in so far as it serves to reinforce certain firmly established and conventional attitudes.

OTHER MEDIA

Propaganda can be disseminated in a thousand ways, but no matter how many novel and ingenious devices are thought up, the mainstay of any campaign will be the spoken and written message, especially as carried by radio and newspaper, but also including public addresses, street-corner meetings, pamphlets, circulars, newsletters and posters. Although the other devices have their value, they are essentially auxiliary media and can be discussed here in very brief summary.

Songs and music have long played an important part in mass movements, particularly among otherwise inarticulate groups. Whenever songs such as "The Internationale," "The Red Flag," "The Marseillaise," "Rule Britannia," or "Dixie" are sung, they remind the singers of their heritage, of battles fought, of difficulties overcome, or of the unity of the cause. Others, the songs of labor movements, of temperance workers, of prisoners, of the exiled, and of oppressed peoples everywhere, have helped to recruit supporters, to arouse sympathy, to counteract the feelings of despair, to encourage or to inspire with hope for a new and happier future. A common weakness of authoritarian regimes is to be so impressed with the propaganda value of song and music as to be unable to recognize it as having any other role. "Only the national element and what appeals to the masses is virile and constitutes real art." [29] In Germany, Dr. Goebbels finally recognized that if propaganda became too intensive and too demanding it would fail in its purpose. In March, 1941, he ordered the relaxation of earlier regulation prohibiting the broadcasting of jazz. In explaining his new position he wrote in the *Völkischer Beobachter,*

> Soldiers at the front after a hard battle appreciate what they called "decent music," which means light music, ... People are in general too strained to absorb more than two hours of an exacting programme. If a man who has worked hard for twelve or fourteen hours wants to hear music at all, it must be music which makes no demands on him. [30]

Art has always had and no doubt will continue to have a propaganda function. In some societies in certain periods it has been fashionable for artists to paint purely for their own pleasure or for the private gratification of a patron, but, more often than not, the artist has considered it part of his responsibility to instruct and enlighten. On occasions, the propaganda function of art has dominated the artists' freedom of choice of subject and manner of treatment, usually to the detriment of the intrinsic "eternal" quality of the painting. This was especially true during the French revolutionary period when the didactic purpose of art was commonly held to be the sole measure of its value. [31] This

stress on art as propaganda has been revered and strengthened in the modern authoritarian regimes. It is the inspiration behind the "Soviet realism" movement in Russia
where all art is to be used "in the interests of the ideological education of the masses." [32]

The chief purpose of uniforms and costumes is to
separate the "select" from the "outsiders": to give the
members of the group a visible symbol of their common
identity, not only with those who wear the uniform now,
but also with those who have worn it in the past. Army
commanders have long recognized the value of morale and
fighting spirit of a distinctive uniform or variation in
uniform for a regiment with long and honorable traditions.
Uniforms serve the further purpose of giving the wearer
an aura of authority. The official costumes of monarchs,
judges, and witch doctors are symbolic of power and
majesty, identifying the individual with the traditions of
his office, thereby according his words a respect they
could not otherwise have.

Symbols such as the cross, the swastika, the hammer and
sickle, or the fasces, together with flags and banners, serve
much the same purpose as uniforms. They are visible
evidence of a unity of purpose or of a common history.
Used skillfully, they can become an impressive portrayal
of unity and strength, effective in some instances of recruiting new members and in others of intimidating potential
opposition. To be successful, however, the symbol must be
recognized for what it is, and the association of the symbol
with the cause it represents must be immediate and un-
mistakable.

Other devices of propaganda include monumental architecture—such things as war memorials, government offices,
towers, statues, and so on—that are intended to represent
the stability and solid achievements of the regime, its past
glories, and its future promises. Propaganda can also be
made, if not directly through scientific achievement, at
least through the reporting of moon rockets and advances
in medicine. National fairs and exhibitions, visiting ballet
troupes, musicians or singers, exchange of teachers and

students, playing host to international conferences, these things and many more of like kind can be used to increase the prestige of a national government and to build up a general atmosphere of friendship and good will.

Such examples could be continued at great length, but to little advantage. The point has already been made that the dissemination of propaganda allows for endless variation and that the mark of the skilled propagandist is the ability to select the most appropriate means of communication in any particular set of circumstances. The factors he must consider are the subject matter of the campaign, the audience at whom it is directed, the communications techniques available, and the time limit within which the campaign must be conducted.

Five

PSYCHOLOGICAL WARFARE

The disintegration of German morale in the last months of 1918 convinced the Great Powers that propaganda was an effective and relatively cheap weapon of war. Among the Allied leaders the value of propaganda was noted and filed away for future reference while the propaganda agencies themselves were disbanded as part of a general disarmament ushering in the new era of peace. But in Germany, the General Staff, in an attempt to excuse the military defeat, grossly exaggerated the part played by Crewe House and the Committee on Public Information. The Commander in Chief, Erich von Ludendorff, repeatedly declared that the German armies were victorious, but had stopped fighting because civilian morale had been destroyed by Allied propaganda. Stress on the "corruption of the German soul" inspired German sociologists and army psychologists to undertake extensive research into the military possibilities of propaganda. From this and from the experiences of the Russian revolution emerged the modern study of psychological warfare.

It is not to be supposed, of course, that psychological warfare is an invention of German sociologists. The paint and feathers of the Cherokee Indians, the *clamor* or battle cry of the Roman soldiers, and the *auto-da-fé* of the Spanish Inquisition were all forms of psychological warfare. All that is new is the attempt to replace the occasional acts of a few exceptional leaders, or the habitual behavior of warlike peoples, by a continuing coördination of political, military and economic decisions with psychological principles founded on a scientific study of human motivations.

Psychological warfare is more than propaganda. It is propaganda tied in and coördinated with military, political and economic strategy and policy. Psychological warfare is based on the knowledge that the chances of success of a military operation are heightened by the demoralization of the enemy, the realization that while screamers attached to bombs will not add to the material destruction they will undermine the "will to resist." And while psychological tricks may increase military effectiveness, so may a military operation supplement a propaganda campaign. News and pictures of Germany's ruthless destruction of Polish cities were invaluable aids to German propagandists trying to persuade other powers that resistance was not the wisest policy. Military victory can be achieved by the destruction of the enemy's material resources, but the amount of destruction necessary to force the enemy to admit defeat depends upon his will, his determination and his perseverance, all of which can be affected by propaganda.

Psychological warfare may precede or supplement a military campaign, "softening" opposition, sowing discord, doubt, and confusion, preparing the way for the armies. It is in this sense, ". . . an offensive war waged with intellectual and emotional 'weapons' to destroy the power of moral resistance in the enemy's army and civilian population and to diminish enemy prestige in the eyes of neutrals." [1] In our own age, with the world divided into nuclear-armed camps, psychological warfare has assumed new dimensions. It has become a substitute for military action and the only form of warfare which the great powers can afford to wage.

Covering as it does such a wide range of activities, psychological warfare is recognizable only in terms of its objectives. Words and deeds that, by corrupting the morale of the enemy, weaken his willingness to fight; that sow discord in the enemy camp and foster suspicion of the motives of the enemy in his own territory and among neutrals; that, if unable to enlist the active support of neutrals, at least keep them sympathetic and neutral; or that foster resistance movements in territories occupied by the enemy, are all part of what is now termed psychological warfare and anything that promotes any of these ends is a weapon of psychological warfare. Successful waging of psychological warfare demands the combined talents of many specialists including, in addition to writers, broadcasters, and artists, some competent to maintain close liaison with the political and military leaders of their own country, others well versed in the language, culture, and politics of the target country, and still others with training in such fields as psychology, anthropology, and political science.[2]

DEVELOPMENT OF PSYCHOLOGICAL WARFARE AFTER 1914—SOVIET EXPERIENCE

Although the Allies were the first to make significant use of propaganda in wartime, the responsibility for introducing it into the regular conduct of international relations belongs to the Soviet Union. The most obvious reason for this is the ideological basis of communism, the sense of mission which, in the beginning at least, motivated many Bolsheviks. A doctrine that proclaimed the international solidarity of working men would seem to demand that those who professed it should unite in spreading the gospel in unenlightened places.

In the first days of high idealism and revolutionary fervor, the propaganda from Russia was skillfully prepared and reasonably effective. But as the theme from the beginning was the desirability and inevitability of revolution, the immediate short-term success was bought at the price of long-range lack of confidence in the Soviet Union. Several years of the propagation of revolution and the overthrow of established governments resulted in a fixed image inhibiting the effectiveness of later attempts to portray the Soviet Union as a respectable peace-loving nation.

Once it had crushed internal opposition, the Soviet Government realized that its principal rival was, and would remain, the West, and especially the United States. Its campaign against the United States has been presented on three fronts. First, within the Soviet Union it has concentrated on building up a picture of America as a plutocracy in which a few mercenary, ruthless capitalists maintain themselves in fabulous luxury by holding the masses down in abject poverty. Insecurity, unemployment, fear, and the denial of social justice are claimed to be the lot of the average American worker.[3] Although the Soviet Union has always admired American technical achievements, she has always asserted that the products of this technical skill are most unfairly distributed, with the workers being cheated out of what is rightly theirs by a political system which serves only to protect the exploiters.

Second, within the United States, open Communist propaganda, although it did make some converts during the depression years, now makes little impression. Mainly concerned with sowing dissension and lack of confidence in the government, Communist propaganda in the United States today is disseminated largely through "front" organizations and by means of spectacular achievements in the field of science which can be so publicized as to undermine American pride and prestige.

Third, Soviet propaganda has worked assiduously to undermine American good will in neutral countries. America has been portrayed as a vast armed camp restrained from imperialist aggression only by fear of Russian retaliation. Neutrals have been told that it is only the Soviet Union that saves them from incorporation in the "Coca-Cola Empire." Every heavy-handed action by American diplomats and businessmen abroad has been grist to the Soviet propaganda mill, increasing tension between America and her allies and undermining the value of technical and economic aid programs. But undoubtedly the greatest asset of Soviet propagandists is racial segregation. The outbursts of the more extreme Southern segregationists are not typical of American opinion. But they can be taken out of context by the Communists and freely broadcast throughout Africa and Asia where they are the one factor most likely to swing the new nations of the world from the democracies into the Communist camp.

In its actual operation Russian propaganda has been characterized by a distinctive use of language described, with fair accuracy, as "semantic warfare."

> The language of Communism . . . is not so much a means of explaining to the unbeliever what Communism means, but an armoury of weapons and tools intended to produce support or dissolve opposition to Communist policies on the part of people either hostile or indifferent to them. The meaning of a Communist word is not what you think it says, but what effect it is intended to produce.[4]

One of the several forms of this special language is the creation of a new vocabulary of compacted words with restricted connotations: *Comintern, Politburo, Gosplan, Comsomol* and so on; words parodied, but not exaggerated by George Orwell in *1984. Miniluv* and *prolefeed* may be part of the vocabulary of Orwell's *Newspeak*, but they would not be foreign to the language of communism.

In addition to their characteristic "special" vocabulary, which also includes a colorful, but highly stylized, brand of invective, the Communists use familiar words and phrases, but they use them in a particular way, often deliberately distorting their reference to confuse both home and foreign opinion. "Peaceful Coexistence," for example, carries to western minds the connotation of toleration and mutual respect, an attitude of "live and let live." In Marxist terminology, however, peace demands the disappearance of the causes of class struggle, so that "peaceful coexistence" implies a world-wide "classless" Communist society. When eighty-one Communist parties met in Moscow in December, 1960, they publicly announced that "peaceful coexistence" meant "the intensification of the struggle of the working class for the triumph of socialist ideas," rather than "the conciliation of bourgeois ideologies." Again, "democracy" is a prestige word; so the Soviet satellites become democracies, but "Peoples' Democracies" to distinguish them from the "decadent bourgeois democracies" of the West.

When the Soviet Union advocates democracy, it is advocating a proletarian democracy uncontaminated by remnants of the Capitalist class. "Colonialism" is *ipso facto* a product of Capitalist imperialism and is not to be confused with a Soviet-inspired national liberation movement.

The Communists use language to build up stereotyped images of friends and foes. Soviet propaganda policy does not allow for subtle shades of friendship. The world is divided into two mutually exclusive camps where those who are not unquestionably loyal are mortal enemies. Neutrals and "deviationists" are left in a difficult position. Denounced one day as the lackeys of imperialism, hailed the next as allies in the struggle for peace, they may find on the third day that the Soviet Union has become the protector of their right to independence and self-determination. Changes of position are accomplished, sometimes by gradual transitions, but more often by the dramatic exposure of sinister plotting or by restitution after the "false accusations of the real enemies of the people."

Such a dichotomous approach to the international scene can be sustained only by an elaborate state apparatus and the institution of a "closed society." (This is described more fully in the next chapter.) The life of the Soviet citizen must be so regimented that no glimmer of contrary attitudes can enter, and the influence of the state must become so catholic in application that at every point the official attitudes are confirmed and reinforced.

> The Soviet citizen can do little to escape the propaganda din, for it follows him into the schoolroom, library, cinema, army barracks and sports arena. He depends for recreation on sports clubs and "palaces of culture," where he is directed into Communist discussion groups and drama circles, sent on excursions to Soviet museums and patriotic shrines, or induced into a reading program in the "Lenin corners." Even the parks of "culture and rest" confront him with propaganda billboards, blaring loudspeakers, and organized entertainment containing the inevitable "message." As in all totalitarian societies, privacy and private absorptions are poorly valued and, wherever possible, are overwhelmed by public purposes.[5]

The strategy of Soviet psychological warfare cannot immediately be discerned from the content of Russian propaganda. Rather, as with the language of propaganda, it can be understood only in the context of formal adherence to Marxist-Leninist ideology. Internal shifts and contradictions are not seen as the aimless vacillations of muddled thinking, but are facets of an attempt, not always successful, at rigid doctrinal consistency. Within the Soviet Union certain assumptions are axiomatic: the triumph of communism has been ordained by history, but eventual victory is being delayed and obstructed by the reactionary policies of the Capitalist powers, therefore the Soviet Union must protect the inheritance of the proletariat from those who would destroy it. This ideological foundation provides a sort of inner logic to such dramatic changes in Soviet policy as the flirtation with Hitler or the retreat from the Stalin cult. Nor was the Soviet Union being inconsistent in its strategical aims when, in 1934, it took a seat on the Council of the League of Nations after years of condemning the League as a tool of imperialism. With the same broad policy in mind, the Communist parties of Asia that, in the immediate postwar period had directed their energies to fomenting the revolution by sabotage, military terrorism and general obstruction of established governments, have in more recent years concluded that indigenous nationalist movements are more immediately damaging to Western influence than the subversive Communist movements and so have offered their loyal support in campaigns to rid their countries of "the last remnants of colonial imperialism."

These tactical shifts in policy, often, of course, based on poor information and a misunderstanding of the West, are intended to support an unchanging strategical aim which is most clearly seen in the Soviet Union's formal relations with the machinery of international communism. In 1919, the Third International (the Comintern) was created to turn the Bolshevik victory in Russia into a world-wide Communist triumph. In 1935, however, the Seventh Congress of the Comintern agreed to "suspend agitation for world revolution in favor of achieving a 'united Front' with the Social Democratic parties of the West against fascism." [6] The Comintern thereafter remained passive until 1943 when, in order to allay Western fears of Communist subversion and to further the unity of the anti-Fascist alliance, it was formally dissolved.

Later, in 1947, once the East-West honeymoon was over, a successor to the Comintern, the Communist Information Bureau, or Cominform, was set up specifically to coördinate the activities of European Communist parties in opposition to the European recovery program and, by agitation and strike action, to keep the Western powers confused and divided. This was one of the more serious blunders of Soviet psychological warfare for its immediate effect was to stiffen Western resistance to further Soviet expansion and to inspire the creation of the NATO military alliance. Certainly it would seem that at least by 1950 the Soviet Union should have begun to retreat from an obstructive attitude that was serving only to strengthen anti-Soviet opinion. The conciliatory note in Russia's public pronouncements for foreign consumption, which followed Stalin's death, did not mean, however, any basic change in policy. Although the Cominform was disbanded in 1956, the objective is still a Communist world under Russian leadership; but the means of achieving this world are disguised, albeit sometimes rather thinly, under the cloak of peaceful cooperation with all men of good will. When, for example, representatives of the Communist parties of sixty-four states met in Moscow in November, 1957, they issued a manifesto calling for world peace, but (and here the disguise was very thin) peace to be brought about by unity and popular support against "Capitalist monopolies that have a vested interest in war" and by the "liquidation of military blocs and bases."

It should not, of course, be assumed that simply because Soviet psychological warfare is founded on a more or less consistent and relatively stable basic program that it has always been successful or that the tactical shifts have all, in fact, led in the direction of the underlying strategy. The determination with which the "ultimate destiny" is pursued and the disciplined coördination of day-to-day operations gives the Soviet Union certain marked advantages. An authoritarian regime, however, places heavy responsibility on one man, and there is still room for such disastrous errors of judgment as Stalin's intransigent obstructionism which united the non-Communist world. The Soviet Union understands the nature and power of psychological warfare and is skilled in its use. But the Russians are not as skilled as they sometime pretend to be nor as powerful as some pessimists in the West assume.

THE DEVELOPMENT OF PSYCHOLOGICAL WARFARE AFTER 1914—GERMAN EXPERIENCE

German propaganda in World War I had been un-believably inept. Stolid military bureaucrats were put in charge of offices staffed by inexperienced amateurs. The result was a series of ponderous unimaginative and un-realistic communiqués which failed to intimidate Germany's enemies and damaged her cause in neutral countries.

As mentioned earlier, Germany's failure in the prop-aganda war was the immediate source of its postwar interest in propaganda. As early as 1921, E. Stern-Rubarth[7] was enunciating the principles later elaborated by Hitler. The first lesson was that propaganda was worthless in isola-tion; it had to be used in conjunction with military, diplo-matic, and economic moves. One of Germany's greatest weaknesses had been the refusal of the different groups engaged in propaganda to coördinate their policies, or even to consult one another. Second, there were serious defects in a propaganda structure based on a fixed, stationary policy too unwieldy for ready adaptation to the changing course of events. In a later era, the ease with which Goebbels' machine accomplished the two transitions of the brief Russian-German alliance of 1940-41 showed the advantages of a single, yet flexible, propaganda organiza-tion.

Adolf Hitler was not an original theorist of propaganda

techniques, but he was a good student who, before applying his lessons, could rephrase them in popular language. "Propaganda," he wrote, "is a truly frightful weapon in the hands of an expert." And the emphasis was on the expert. According to the doctrines of National Socialism only the leader, the expert, knew what was good for the masses and only he was really qualified to teach them. Propaganda for the masses had to be simple, reduced to easily learned slogans, repeated over and over again, concentrating on such basic emotional elements as love and hatred.

> The great masses receptive ability is only very limited, their understanding is small, but their forgetfulness is great. As a consequence of these facts, all effective propaganda has to limit itself only to a very few points and to use them like slogans until even the very last man is able to imagine what is intended by such a word.[8]

Hitler's practical success as a propagandist followed largely from his awareness of the need to coördinate propaganda and action. As he wrote in *Mein Kampf,* the prime purpose of propaganda was to win new supporters for the organization and the first task of the organization was to win new people for the continuation of propaganda. Propaganda and organization, words and deeds, were inseparably bound together. Thus, when the film version of Erich Maria Remarque's novel *All Quiet on the Western Front* was released in Berlin in 1930, the Nazis were not content simply to attack it in print. On the second day of its screening Goebbels issued tickets to a gang of S. A. hooligans who released white mice and set off stink bombs in the cinema. The next day the government withdrew the film to prevent further rioting.[9] This understanding of the relationship between propaganda and action was apparent even in the first days of the Nazi movement. While Hitler was struggling for power, for example, gangs of young Nazis were ordered to march with uniforms and banners into hostile Marxist districts to provoke street fights, in order to draw attention to the movement and to attract to its ranks the mobster element from cities. Their own casualties were publicized as martyrs to the cause of a greater, nobler Germany. When legal action was brought against the libelous Nazi party paper, *Der Angriff*, Goebbels was delighted at the additional publicity. He regarded the police courts as places where he could show off his insolence and gain some space for himself in the papers of his rivals.[10]

Uniforms, bands, flags, symbols were all part of the German propaganda machine, designed by Hitler and Goebbels to increase the impact of strong words by evidence of strong deeds. Meetings were not just occasions for people to make speeches, they were carefully planned theatrical productions in which settings, lighting, background music, and the timing of entrances and exits were devised to maximize the emotional fervor of an audience already brought to fever pitch by an hour or more given over to singing and the shouting of slogans. Describing the setting of Hitler's broadcast speech at Nuremberg, September 15, 1938, Serge Chakotin wrote:

> On a foundation of Wagnerian music there was heard a daunting rumbling, slow and emphatic, of drums and heavy footfalls pounding the earth, together with an indescribable rattle and swish and pant of armed masses on the march. This noise, now growing, now receding, must have clutched at the hearts of the millions of listeners, filling them with apprehension of disaster, a feeling of fascination and fear, deliberately produced by the men who staged the spectacle.[11]

The main objective of Hitler's internal domestic program was to unify the German people, to create one people with but a single thought, a single fixed purpose. This in turn became the principal element of the psychological warfare campaign launched against those whom Hitler wished to conquer, this stress on the invincibility of a united and determined nation. The determination not only to be united, but to give public testimony of unity, was to a large extent the rationale behind the constant display of Nazi symbols.

It must be the duty of each fellow-citizen who professes his allegiance to our Leader, to demonstrate his loyalty by adorning his dwelling on election day with the symbol of the New Germany, the Swastika flag. There must be no house which does not display the sign of National Socialist Germany.[12]

The same rationale lay behind orders insisting on the use by all public officials of the *Heil Hitler* salute and the coördination of all cultural activities (a term which embraced literature, the press, films, the theater, the arts, music, and broadcasting, including all who serviced these activities) under the Reich Chamber of Culture. The schools were not concerned only with the propagation of the Nazi ideology as a set of beliefs. They were also adapted to the specific requirements of a military upbringing so that, whenever possible, a military slant was given to all courses of instruction. Arithmetic, for example, was taught in terms of military science, with problems being drawn from ballistics and the movements of soldiers, tanks, and bombs rather than from commerce and the filling of bathtubs.

While the guiding objective of all propaganda within Germany was unity, the motivation of the psychological warfare campaign launched against foreign countries was disunity and confusion. It was the avowed intention of the Nazi propagandists to seek out and intensify all the latent frictions within any society they proposed to attack. The Nazis and their friends in foreign countries delighted in stirring up racial antagonisms, implanting suspicion and distrust of government, exacerbating labor-management differences, encouraging every disruptive and fragmentary cause, fostering religious hatreds, supporting any and every movement likely to obstruct any other nation's attempt to achieve the unity of will that was the objective of Nazi domestic policy. In the cause of weakening through division, old international fears, jealousies, and hates were revived. Frenchmen were reminded of what they had been told in the First World War, that "England would fight to the last Frenchman." The English were warned that the French were unreliable allies. Australians, Canadians and New Zealanders were told that England regarded them as inferior colonials, fit only for "cannon fodder."

A major achievement of German psychological warfare was to convince the democracies that Germany was a peaceful country, forced by necessity to occupy certain territories such as Czechoslovakia and the Saarland. The democracies were also somehow persuaded that each successive occupation was Germany's "last territorial claim in Europe." As late as August, 1938, General Sir Ian Hamilton is quoted as saying, "The Germans are much more active for peace than Britons, and firmly believe that Herr Hitler can keep them out of war. . . . I am sure the Fuehrer is horrified at the idea of a European war." [13] The Munich Agreement, signed by Adolf Hitler and Neville Chamberlain in September, 1938, reads, in part, "We regard the agreement signed last night and the Anglo-German Naval Agreement as symbolic of the desire of our two peoples never to go to war with one another." This is perhaps the greatest triumph of German psychological warfare.

PSYCHOLOGICAL WARFARE IN
WORLD WAR II

The War of 1939-45 provided opportunity for new developments in psychological warfare as a military weapon; a triple-pronged weapon intended first of all to demoralize the enemy's soldiers, then to undermine the will to resist throughout the enemy country, and finally, a defensive weapon to sustain the spirit of one's own forces against similar psychological attacks by the enemy.

The role of psychological warfare in wartime has been very clearly set out in a directive issued jointly by the principal allied propaganda organizations, the British Political Warfare Executive (PWE) and the American Office of War Information (OWI). This directive stated that psychological warfare was "not a magic substitute for physical battle, but an auxiliary to it." Its purpose was to "reduce the cost of the physical battle" and make it easier to deal with the enemy after surrender, and it was to do this by attacking the fighting morale of the enemy. It was the "task of Psychological Warfare to assist the Supreme Commander in fulfilling his mission against the enemy with the most economical use of troops and equipment." But it was to be remembered that psychological warfare had to be waged in the context of general government policy, and while policy would not define the immediate strategy of psychological attacks, it would set limits within which such strategy would have to be confined.[14] It will be recalled from Chapter Three that this need to coördinate propaganda and policy was one of the main concerns of the Inter-Allied Propaganda Conference held in London in February, 1918. The same concern appears several times in the diaries of Dr. Goebbels, although in this case, Goebbels was less worried about adapting his propaganda campaigns to the general policy of his government than he was with trying to gain greater influence in policy formulation in order to prevent it from conflicting with his propaganda campaigns.

There are several ways for dividing the subject of psychological warfare for closer study, but perhaps the most useful is according to the campaign objectives. This would follow the threefold division mentioned above where propaganda has the immediate aim of destroying the morale of the enemy's fighting forces, the more long-term strategic aim of breaking the will to resist throughout the enemy's country, and the defensive aim of protecting one's own soldiers against enemy propaganda.

The principal weapons of immediate tactical propaganda against the enemy's forces, "combat propaganda," as it is sometimes called, are leaflets, various forms of broadcasting, and terror tactics. Of these the most widely used is the leaflet, especially the invitation to surrender combined with the safe-conduct pass. The surrender of the enemy is, after all, the basic aim of combat propaganda. After two world wars the major powers have learned a lot about this form of propaganda. No one now expects a soldier to use a safe-conduct pass while he has any realistic hope of victory or escape. The fact that some soldiers pick up surrender leaflets and hide them away is always regarded by Intelligence as the first hopeful sign that the "will to resist" is beginning to weaken. The surrender leaflet is not a substitute for military victory, but it may lower the cost of that victory by persuading the enemy that life as a prisoner of war is preferable to death. It will only be effective when the enemy believes that the alternatives are death or prison camp or when he fears further battle more than he fears his own officers. Even then, the soldier may choose death, or be persuaded by his officers to choose death, if he cannot live with "honor." So the modern leaflet speaks, not of "surrender," but of "coming over." It does not threaten or issue ultimata, but warns and invites; it resists the temptation to call the enemy a coward or a knave and addresses him as a brave man yielding only when all hope is gone.[15]

A common mistake of many leaflets is to ask of the enemy more than he can reasonably be expected to do. One Soviet leaflet told the German troops that if they wished to save Germany they would have to overthrow Hitler, a task so beyond the ability of the ordinary German soldier that his reaction could only be one of anger against those who required it of him. The Russians achieved much greater success with a series of leaflets ostensibly issued either by the German government or by the Nazi party, skillfully imitating the style and format of German bulletins. In content each contained only one or two points embarrassing to the Nazi regime in the midst of other material which could quite easily have been German in origin. These were regarded as sufficiently dangerous for Goebbels to take special measures to counteract them.[16]

These Russian leaflets achieved their purpose largely because the German soldiers were deceived about their point of origin, but such successful deception is not easy. Japanese leaflets, for example, could seldom be mistaken for anything other than Japanese, for the idiom always rang false and the slang, when it was used, was generally twenty years or more out of date. Indeed, experience soon showed that if one could not be sure of hoodwinking the enemy it was safer not to try. For this reason, the British broadcasters found that if they did not pretend to be anything but English, speaking German with an unmistakably English accent, they received a more sympathetic hearing than when they used German announcers. A genuine German voice from a British broadcasting station prompted the question, "What's he doing over there? He can only be a traitor," and the emotional disturbances aroused by the concept of a traitor were likely to drown out any impact the message might have made.

Leaflets and terror are not entirely separate forms of propaganda, although terror covers a wider range of activity. The incitement of fear is still, however, one of the major aims of the leaflet writer. A typical leaflet dropped by the American forces over the German lines during the latter part of the war was headed "WHEN ALL HELL BREAKS LOOSE" and went on to describe "uninterrupted barrages," "continuous dive-bombing," "carpets of bombs," "new flame throwers" and promised "Tomorrow: Hell!" [17] Following heavy Allied raids on Germany, Goebbels ordered that pictures of the shattered cities of Lübeck and Rostock be dropped over Britain, with the warning that the British must now expect reprisal raids of equal ferocity.

Terror itself is the oldest form of psychological warfare. It is the inspiration behind the feathers and paint of the warring tribesmen and the screamers on the diving *Stuka* bombers. In the early campaigns of the war the Nazis made particularly effective use of terror. Just before they invaded Norway, for example, they arranged for Norwegian officials to see a film of the Polish campaign. The film demonstrated the full horror of mechanized war with endless lines of tanks and armored cars, cities erupting under a rain of bombs, dead and injured women and children, all the noise, speed, and shock of modern war. The constant theme of German propaganda, up until 1942 at least, was that "this is what has happened to others, it's now about to happen to you!" Throughout the campaign in France, German agents added to the terror and confusion with rumors, contradictory news reports, stories of the collapse and surrender of French units, of betrayal by France's allies, of the corruption and cupidity of her government, and of the ruthless efficiency of the German military machine. The endless streams of refugees who hindered the movement of Allied troops and equipment were in part the victims of German terror propaganda.

Strategic psychological warfare is a term broad enough to embrace a tremendous range of activities. It can include German efforts to keep alive and intensify differences of opinion between the British government and the Indian Congress party in 1942,[18] and the attempts of the Allies to divide the German people from the Nazi party. On this latter point it is interesting to note several references in the diaries of Dr. Goebbels in which he welcomed the outbursts of the more extreme Germanophobes, such as Lord Vansittart, who repeatedly urged the destruction of the entire German people, for such attacks could only drive the Germans closer to the party. The skilled propagandist should exploit every possible source of friction within the enemy ranks. Properly handled, even Russian victories could be an asset to the German propagandists. The Fuehrer, said Goebbels, approved his tactics of letting reports of Russian advances go out to the world unchallenged. "Let Europe get the creeps; all the sooner will it become sensible. Besides, our anti-Bolshevik propaganda is the apple of discord in the enemy camp." [19]

A major strategic effort of Allied psychological warfare was to commit the enemy to one specific task that was possibly beyond him: the defense of the Atlantic Wall at all costs. By exaggerating the strength of the German defense and stressing its importance to German security the Allies doubled the shock to German public opinion when it was finally breached and at the same time prepared a state of mind where their own failure would not have appeared so disastrous or unexpected.[20] Preparations to soften the blow of possible defeat are not, of course, new. Walter Lippmann has described the manner in which the communiqués before the battle of Verdun were drafted. Hope was raised by stressing the determination and strength of the French forces, but at the same time stress on the gigantic and unprecedented effort about to be launched by the German forces implied the possibility of defeat.[21] Emphasis on the strength of the enemy makes victory more glorious and defeat less shameful.

Psychological warfare is concerned with such things as the encouragement of resistance movements in enemy occupied countries and, what is psychologically even more important, keeping the enemy tense and nervous about the possibility of sabotage and attack by the resistance forces. A broadcast from SHAEF radio in May, 1944, for example, was intended as much for the German forces as for the civilians in occupied Europe, although it was addressed ostensibly only to the latter. It asked the people in the occupied countries to gather information about the enemy, to "observe the number of men and of vehicles by type," and to note "their arms and their arrangements for the supply of food and petrol." Civilians were asked to note the appearance of senior officers and leaders among their civilian supporters. They were to find out the names of these people and to note "when they come and go and where they go to." They were to look for points where water and lighting systems might be destroyed, and finally they were asked to be "patient above all, and hide all your actions until the word is given." [22] Broadcasts of this kind not only encourage one's friends and needle the enemy, they force the enemy to divert men and materials to discovering and frustrating resistance movements.

A variation on the "preparation for liberation" theme was tried, apparently with some success, in northern Burma. Each leaflet became a small packet with a token gift, a packet of seeds or salt, a few matches, or needles and thread, with a message of hope, or instructions on how to sabotage Japanese installations. Some seed packets bore the slogan, "Wherever the Japanese go, they bring destruction. Wherever the Allied forces come, the fields spring up green." [23] But whatever the technique adopted, and we have here merely noted a few from a seemingly endless list of tricks, the aims are the same: confusion, doubt, fear, and despair in the enemy camp, courage and hope among one's defeated Allies, and good will among neutrals.

The enemy is, of course, engaged in the same sort of enterprise and psychological warfare must be as much concerned with defense as with attack. The form of such defensive propaganda is obvious and requires at this stage little elaboration for it is not much more than the denial and refutation of the enemy's charges. It requires efforts to build up unity, to resist the enemy's attempts to incite racial, national, political, or economic conflict within one's own country, to demonstrate that victory is certain, but not so certain that effort can be relaxed, to make it clear that the cause is indeed worth the sacrifices demanded, that the leaders have the "good of the people" at heart and to show that one's Allies are worthy of the confidence placed in them. That the attempt to give practical application to these general principles requires constant surveillance and a painstaking eye for detail is clear from three small items. First, after a particularly heavy raid on Berlin at the end of 1943, army units were called in to help clear the streets and it so happened that the only transport vehicles available were tanks. Dr. Goebbels commented in his diary:

> I saw to it that the tanks were withdrawn to the Berlin barracks by morning, otherwise we would certainly have read in the enemy press the following day that the Nazis had to call upon the *Wehrmacht* to protect themselves from the furious people! And so one has to pay attention to a thousand big and a thousand small things.[24]

The second item is a letter written by Mr. Churchill to his Secretary of State for War:

> Now is the time to popularize your administration with the troops by giving all regiments and units the little badges and distinctions they like so much. I saw the London Irish with their green and peacock-blue hackles. We can easily afford the expense of bronze badges, the weight of which is insignificant in metal. All regimental distinctions should be encouraged.[25]

This third item, also a letter from Winston Churchill, shows more than the other two the concern for names and labels, the "appearance of things."

> I hope the term "Communal Feeding Centres" is not going to be adopted. It is an odious expression suggestive of Communism and the workhouse. I suggest you call them "British Restaurant." Everybody associates the word "restaurant" with a good meal, and they may as well have the name if they cannot get anything else.[26]

GROWTH OF PSYCHOLOGICAL WARFARE IN THE WEST

Even a superficial survey of the political influences at work in a democratic society leads to the obvious conclusion that propaganda is being disseminated from a thousand sources through every media of communication. The press, the educational system, the motion picture and the theater, radio and television, books and periodicals, the graphic arts, and all other propaganda techniques are used in all countries, either by government agencies or private institutions, for the furthering of political causes.

But although it might be impossible to identify techniques as characteristic of democratic or non-democratic propaganda, it is still obvious that the character of propaganda in a democracy differs from that in a dictatorship. The precise nature of the difference is not, however, quite so obvious. No one seriously disputes the fact that in a modern dictatorship propaganda plays a much larger role as a deliberate instrument of official policy than it does in a democracy. Yet there is probably a greater volume of propaganda in the United States today than there ever was in Hitler's Germany. It is less dominating, however, less overpowering and therefore less evident, because it originates not in one source, but in hundreds. It is disseminated by political parties, trade unions, churches, business houses, newspaper owners, government departments, politicians, societies, clubs, professional associations, and individuals. It is at this level that the difference between democratic and non-democratic propaganda becomes apparent. The average citizen in a democracy seems to have no objection to political propaganda as such, and seems to regard as legitimate almost any method of political persuasion short of direct corruption and intimidation, provided, however, that it is not done by the government. This last point is all important. In a dictatorship all propaganda is government propaganda; in a democracy there is great reluctance to allow the government to enter into the propaganda field at all.

This distrust of government propaganda explains the pressure on any democratic country to withdraw from the propaganda field as soon as the immediate crisis of war is over. But because, in the years immediately following the end of World War II, the United States government demobilized its wartime psychological warfare facilities,[27] it had to build up a completely new organization to cope with the Cold War. Remobilization followed as the Western world began to appreciate the changed character of postwar international politics. Beginning slowly in 1948, and speeding up after the outbreak of the Korean conflict in 1950, the United States government has now established a complex organization for international psychological warfare.

The Department of State, through its Bureau of Public Affairs (Office of News) provides, through all the major media of communication, a world-wide news coverage of the activities of the United States government in foreign affairs, and generally announces and explains the foreign policy of the country. More specifically in the realm of international propaganda is the United States Information Agency established in 1953. Guided by the decisions of the Department of State and the National Security Council, its function is "to submit evidence to the peoples of other nations by means of communications techniques that the objectives and policies of the United States are in harmony with and advance their legitimate aspirations for freedom, progress and peace."[28] Outside the United States, the Agency's offices, integral parts of the various American embassies and consulates, are known as the United States Information Service (USIS). There are now USIS offices in more than eighty countries, all charged with interpreting and explaining the policies of the United States government, countering "hostile attempts to distort or frustrate the objectives and policies of the United States," [29] and generally presenting a picture of the life and culture of the American people that will facilitate understanding of American policies and objectives.

The official psychological warfare of the Western powers is generally tactically sound, for the propagandists have taken to heart a lesson from the First World War: the principle that all good propaganda must be factually true, that one should never make statements that might later be refuted. And it is important that material should not only be true, it should also be credible. M. F. Herz, who was for a time working with the combat propaganda team attached to the Fifth Army in Italy during World War II, recalls the disastrous effects of American propaganda leaflets in which it was mentioned that prisoners in American P.O.W. camps received eggs for breakfast. This, although perfectly true, seemed so preposterous to the enemy that they rejected it and so were inclined to disbelieve the rest of the message. The leaflets had to be withdrawn.[30]

Another important lesson, more fully appreciated by those engaged in psychological warfare than by those voting the money for it, is that psychological warfare is not just large-scale advertising. International persuasion is a complex matter requiring an understanding of the attitudes of those whose attention is sought, and the advertising techniques, which work so well in the American marketplace, are not necessarily appropriate in countries with different standards of values. "What sells soap in Indiana can unsell democracy in India." A successful psychological warfare campaign requires a detailed background study of the aspirations and values of the country concerned. It is necessary to know the attitudes of the country towards the United States, the other Western countries, the Soviet

Union, and the neutral countries; and the factors, favorable and unfavorable, that would affect United States propaganda activities. These would include the source, nature, and strength of other influences on public opinion, the communication channels available, and the nature and causes of differences of opinion within the country.

It is useless to dwell on the virtues of free private enterprise in underdeveloped lands where the doctrines of laissez faire have never taken root. Little advantage is gained by providing economic aid, unless there is tight control of associated publicity. The propagandist must know his foreign country. Too often American generosity has failed to achieve its purpose because Soviet propagandists have been able to create the image of "sinister dollar imperialism," the "underwriting of the forces of reaction," or of American duplicity in using the small nations as pawns in the struggle against the Soviet Union. The United States has not always been quick or effective in replying to these charges.

Many mistakes are made in psychological warfare, by anti-democratic forces as well as by the West, through a misinterpretation of audience reaction. An American radio station, for example, might receive enthusiastic reports of a program beamed to a Russian-occupied country, but there would be grave danger in placing too much reliance on such reports without first "weighing" them. That is to say, the opinion of right-wing opponents of a Communist regime is not of much value in assessing the effectiveness of propaganda aimed at Communist sympathizers. Propaganda should be directed at the "marginal" man, "the man who does not believe everything we say, but who is interested in our message because he does not believe everything our opponents say either." [31] American propaganda makes little, or no, impact on the dedicated Communist and for the convinced anti-Communist the effort is unnecessary. Its target is, or should be, the waverer. The enthusiasm with which it is received in the anti-Communist camp is usually a poor measure of its accuracy in hitting that target.

THE "COLD WAR"

Psychological warfare was specifically developed as an aid to military action, to make victory more certain and to reduce the cost of armed conflict. Since 1945, however, psychological warfare has undergone a transformation. It has continued unabated, perhaps even at times intensified, but as a substitute for, rather than an auxiliary to, military engagement.

It is, however, an oversimplificaton to think of the Cold War as just the latest in history's apparently endless series of conflicts, differing only in that conventional arms have been replaced by psychological weapons. The Cold War is being conducted between two ideological divisions, one of which regards conflict as the normal state of affairs between nations. To the Communist "the history of all hitherto existing society is the history of class struggles," struggles which can cease only when the class basis of society is itself eliminated. From this basic assumption, axiomatic to all good Communists, it follows that, unlike earlier wars, there can be no agreed cessation of hostilities in the Cold War, no compromise solution for the maintenance of the status quo. According to Marxist theory, the continuation of class conflict is the status quo. If the West is to survive, it must recognize that the Cold War will continue; for it can end only with the final victory of one side, which seems unlikely in any foreseeable future, or in a shooting war, a nuclear war, in which there may be no victor.

For a brief period after the armistice in 1945, it seemed possible that the good will and fellowship of the military alliance might continue; but within a year all illusions, except among a number of naïve idealists, were destroyed. With its rejection of the Baruch plan for the control of atomic weapons in June, 1946, the Soviet Union made it clear that it was not going to cooperate with the West. Instead, the Soviet Union initiated a policy of fomenting discord and encouraging revolutionary Communist movements in all countries outside the direct control of Russia. The ruthlessness and determination with which this policy was conducted finally roused the West to take counteraction and, beginning in March, 1947, a combination of military aid, economic support, and moral encouragement checked Soviet advances in Greece and halted further expansion in the Balkans.

The assumptions on which Soviet psychological warfare is based, when applied to the formulation of foreign policy, demand first of all that the Soviet Union become strong enough to safeguard the revolution from external enemies. Second, it is also necessary that the Soviet Union continue to harry and confuse the West, lending its aid to any movement or group which embarrasses or threatens Western unity, probing and enlarging upon any divisions or discords that may arise among the non-Communist states, and seeking to discredit the major Western powers in Asia, Latin America, and Africa, in the belief that it can thereby weaken the West and hasten the collapse of capitalism. Third, in pursuance of this same policy, the Soviet Union must aid and abet the establishment and continuance of Communist movements and "front" organizations, the "seeds of revolution," whenever and wherever they are likely to be valuable. And finally, in order to preserve unflinching unity of purpose, the Soviet Union insists on rigid "doctrinal purity," launching the bitterest of attacks on those who, while professing to be Communists, deviate from the Moscow line.

Yet a psychological warfare campaign will have the desired effect only if the assumptions on which it is based are themselves soundly established. And for a long time the assumptions on which Soviet policy was based were not founded in fact. With a less dogmatic approach to politics, they could have been recognized as false. It was, for example, assumed that the postwar withdrawal of United States troops from Europe signaled America's return to isolationism. This inspired the attempts to frighten the small powers of Europe into accepting Russian domination, but the actual result was that the United States renounced isolationism and took over the leadership of the Western alliance. It was also taken for granted that the shift of the American economy from a war to a peace basis would be followed by a major economic collapse. This led the Russians to a serious underestimation of the extent to which the United States could assist European economic recovery and the extent to which she could use economic aid as an anti-Communist weapon in underdeveloped countries. The failure to appreciate the resilience of the American economy led further to overconfidence about the role of native Communist parties in exploiting the discontents of the victims of economic crisis. Finally, the Russians believed that British-United States relations would be characterized by increasingly bitter rivalry and took this to mean that organizations such as NATO would be rendered ineffectual and unstable by the antagonisms of the principal members. Frequent attempts by the Soviet Union to exploit natural differences between the two nations have almost inevitably resulted in even closer ties between Britain and America.[32]

In turning now to the Western approach to psychological warfare, we can begin by recalling the reluctance with which democratic societies permit their governments to use official funds and resources for propaganda. Although this is particularly true of domestic party politics, or what might be interpreted as party politics, the same fear of official propaganda extends into the field of international psychological warfare. The great handicap which the West has had to overcome has not been one of moral scruple about the kind of tactics which should be adopted, but the jealousy of private agencies which have been unwilling to give to governments the powers necessary to wage psychological warfare.

The Soviet Union gained tremendous initial advantages in the Cold War because the United States government, unable to convince a parochial and unimaginative Congress of the values of psychological warfare, was for several years unable to obtain the funds necessary to launch any large-scale reply to Soviet claims. In July, 1950, during a Soviet campaign to portray the United States as the aggressor in Korea, President Truman asked Congress "to implement his call for a 'great campaign of truth' by granting a supplemental appropriation of $89 million for foreign information activities." [33] This appropriation was drastically cut by Congress to the extent that the regular and supplemental appropriation totaled only $94 million. Partly explainable in terms of the traditional congressional distrust of the State Department and partly a product of a system of government which sets Congress up as a check on administrative spending, these reduced appropriations reflect, even more, an unwillingness of Congress to invest money in schemes having such intangible objectives as "a more sympathetic attitude to the United States and its policies."

Attacks on the United States psychological warfare campaigns have come therefore from three sources: those who have a vested interest in defeating or obstructing United States policy, the unimaginative and the anti-intellectuals who do not appreciate the potency of psychological warfare and who distrust those engaged in it, and the laissez faire extremists, the determined opponents of any extension of governmental power, who deny the right of the administration to engage in propaganda. These three forces, otherwise so far apart, together hindered for several years the American attempt to compete on equal terms with Soviet propaganda in the international field. The United States did not at first have the resources, nor were those engaged in psychological warfare given sufficient control over policy to ensure consistency in their campaigns.

Much of this initial disadvantage has now been overcome and the West now has financial and technical resources which could be used to overcome an initial disadvantage. It is important to remember this, for there is a tendency to assume that because the West started late in the propaganda struggle, because it has undoubtedly made blunders in Cold War strategy, and because it lacks the tireless persistence of the Soviet bloc, the West must always be defeated. To counter this pessimism it is well to recall that the West won the first really big trial of strength. When the Russians clamped down the blockade on Berlin on April 1, 1948, they clearly thought they could force the West to give up the city. The West replied with the air lift which continued from July, 1948, until the Russians lifted the blockade in May, 1949. The air lift was more than a superb technical achievement; it was evidence of the determination of the Western powers not to be intimidated by Russia. It was the first major setback suffered by the Soviets and it effectively destroyed the myth of their invincibility. The heartening effect of the air lift was followed by a series of treaties and military alliances, from NATO to ANZUS, that refuted Russian charges that the Western countries would soon tear each other to pieces.

In retrospect it would seem that, as long as Soviet Cold War strategy was dominated by Stalin's inflexible dogmatism, the West had a fair chance of victory, but that advantage has for a time slipped away. Soviet policy became more realistic, more adaptable to changing circumstances, while American policy, possibly as a product of McCarthyism, became infected with an anti-Communist hysteria that led the Americans to commit a number of tragic blunders. The principal mistakes of United States Cold War strategy have stemmed from the failure in some high places to understand that the people of Asia and Africa, and even of Europe, see neither communism nor the free enterprise "American way of life" as these might be seen by the right wing of the Republican party or by the Daughters of the American Revolution. When, for example, in January, 1954, John Foster Dulles announced his policy of "massive retaliation to deter aggression," it appeared from European comment that he had scared his Allies more than he had scared the Russians.

Again, it must be pointed out that the successes are not all one-sided, that the Russians have no special magic which ensures that every victory will be theirs. One has only to recall the tremendous blow to Russian prestige that followed the savage and inept handling of the Hungarian uprising and the inability of the Russians to halt the flow of defections from the occupied countries to the West. The wall that divides Berlin is a monument to the

failure of Communist propaganda. So long as the democracies continue to exploit every weakness and failure of the
Russian dictatorship, the Cold War can be turned to the
advantage of the Western powers.

One cannot leave the subject of American psychological warfare without mentioning the extent to which
officially-sponsored campaigns are supplemented, but sometimes also frustrated, by private ventures. Unlike the
dictatorships, where all public communication is government communication, the United States is the home of
hundreds of organizations anxious to have their say in
converting the world to the "American way of life," a
phrase which does not mean the same thing to all Americans everywhere. One of the most influential and well
established of these groups is the American Committee for
Liberation, founded in 1951 by "American individuals
deeply concerned for the future of the Soviet peoples." [34]
The major enterprise of the Committee is Radio Liberation
which maintains a twenty-four-hour-a-day program to the
Soviet Union from nine "national desks"—Russian, Ukrain-
ian, Armenian, Azerbaijanian, Byelorussian, Georgian,
North Caucasian, Tatar-Baskir and Turkestani. Radio
Liberation's headquarters are in Munich and it has trans-
mitters in both Europe and the Far East. "Each desk
endeavors to speak from the point of view of its own
people in support of the common cause." [35] Another
private venture into international broadcast propaganda
is Radio Free Europe, and a parallel organization, Radio
Free Asia. These are, as one writer has expressed it,
"dedicated to broadcasting those things which the State
Department finds it impolitic to put on the air." [36] The
traditions of international protocol impose certain limits
on the sort of thing the officials of one government may
say about the officials of another, but Radio Free Europe
has no need to feel inhibited by such traditions. It has
sometimes been suggested that the State Department does
not object to the existence of Radio Free Europe and that,
perhaps, there is a measure of unofficial cooperation.

American magazines with a wide foreign circulation,

magazines such as *Time, Life, Saturday Evening Post,* and *Reader's Digest* are in obvious medium for American propaganda, but at least as important as the editorial and feature material, which often overstates the case, are the advertisements. These, designed primarily for the American consumer, present to less fortunate peoples an image of sybaritic abundance. The articles may be discounted as "mere propaganda," but the advertisements will impress because they give a "real" picture of the American way of life. This impression of easy luxury is reinforced in the overseas offices of American corporations and official agencies. I have myself spent many afternoons in the USIS Library in London, not only because it was an excellent library, but because on a winter's day it seemed to be one of the few places where one could be sure of being warm.

All this amounts to a massive anti-Communist campaign greatly in excess of anything the government can hope to do and it certainly does much to redress the disadvantages the United States government must suffer in dealing with a totalitarian regime. But these private ventures themselves have one great, insoluble, and perhaps even fatal weakness. By their very nature they are uncoördinated. They frequently contradict each other, they attack communism for a variety of not always consistent reasons, and they often damage United States policy by destroying the image which the government is trying to create, especially in some neutral or uncommitted nation. Those right-wing extremists, for example, who vie with each other in spying out Communists in the most unlikely places, dangerously undermine America's status in Europe as an honest, free democracy, opposed to the Soviet Union not only because it is a rival military and economic power, but because the existence of communism is a threat to political liberty, which America genuinely values.

While in the Cold War all the familiar devices of psychological warfare continue to be used: oral and written propaganda of every kind, winning friends and influencing people through economic or military aid, "front" organizations and the encouragement of friendly movements, and the various tricks and stratagems of international negotiation, there has been one substantial new development. All psychological warfare is based on the determinist theories and conditioning experiments conducted by Pavlov.[37] This much is fairly obvious, but there has been more recently a "refinement" in the techniques of "conditioning" and an extension of their use. This new technique, which has been given the name of "brainwashing," consists first of all of a softening-up process in which the resistance of individuals is broken down by "hunger, fatigue, tenseness, threats, violence," and in extreme cases, drugs and hypnotism.[38] This is followed by an indoctrination process through which the victim is persuaded that he has been let down and betrayed by his former friends, and that his persecutors are in reality the only ones he can trust, the ones who will protect him from further betrayal, his only "true" friends. The horror of brainwashing is its effectiveness in destroying the mind of the individual. The harrowing accounts in Koestler's *Darkness at Noon* or Orwell's *1984* are not purely fictional. They are not unlike the actual treatment of some American prisoners of war in Korea.

There is some evidence that brainwashing tactics can succeed in special cases. Although after the Korean conflict the number of American prisoners who declined to return to the United States was small (one report states that there were only twenty-one out of a total of more than seven thousand who had been captured), this was the first time American prisoners of war had refused to return home.[39] These numbers, of course, fade into insignificance compared with the thousands who have defected from East to West, and although they show that brainwashing can have some impact, they demonstrate even more clearly its limitations. In evidence before the House Committee on Un-American Activities, Edward Hunter made the point that brainwashing succeeds best with those whose intelligence is high, but whose education is low, those whose "heads were like a good, solid, but empty bucket, only waiting to be filled." [40] According to Hunter, the Communists were able to impose their version of American action in Korea because the American forces on the whole lacked any other information about American policy towards communism. He illustrated the types of pressure that could be put on a prisoner by recounting the experiences of one Air Force officer who had been subjected to alternating periods of brutality and care until, to quote the officer, when finally the brutality ceased, ". . . you are grateful to them for saving your life. You forget that they are the people who almost killed you." [41]

Although the Communists have had notable success in psychological warfare, especially among the "propertyless, resentful, politically unenfranchised, frustrated, mentally underdeveloped masses of mankind," [42] it is easy to over-estimate their ability, a misjudgment almost as dangerous to the West as the complete disregard of the psychological struggle. In giving too much stress to Soviet Cold War victories, there is a tendency to overlook those Communist advances which are due, not to propaganda, but to skillful deployment of force, careful party organization, and the determination to make the most of every opportunity. With great skill the Russians have managed to seize the popular role of "apostle of peace," forcing the West into the embarrassing position of refusing to take part in "peace movements" and having to condemn all peace campaigns as Communist fronts. The extent to which "peace" became a Communist monopoly was illustrated by a cartoon by Giles of the London *Daily Express*. In the picture, one little urchin is chalking something on the sidewalk, the other is yelling at the top of his voice, "Mum, Cyril's wrote a wicked word." The "wicked word" is PEECE. [43] But this type of triumph is rare. Much Russian propaganda is characterized by a battering-ram technique and a crude repetition of dull, meaningless dogmatism.

Against this intellectual strait jacket of Marxism the democracies have many advantages. Their message, properly presented, offers greater hope and greater respect for human dignity and individual well-being. The Western powers, apart from a few embarrassing allies whose only virtue is a determined anti-communism, have an impressive record of social and material progress. In most there is a substantial body of human rights and freedoms, reasonably well protected by law and custom. The major Western powers have also the advantage of an abundant supply of raw materials that, combined with a highly advanced technology, ensure both a material standard of living and a war-making potential that would not easily be challenged. The West has thus a good case to make in the Cold War, and access to a network of communications for presenting this case to the world. All that is required is an awareness of the nature of the Cold War and its near-permanent character, and a sense of determination to continue it. Given these there is no reason to suppose that the West must lose nor that it need abandon its own values in fighting that war.

Six

PROPAGANDA IN TWO SOCIETIES

THE VOLUME OF PROPAGANDA

Although propaganda emerged as one of the consequences of granting formal political power to the people[1] its use obviously has not been confined to the democracies. The concept of "government by the people" has acquired universal status and prestige so that even within the major authoritarian regimes a great deal of time and effort is now devoted to gaining the appearance of the popular support of the masses who would simply have been ignored in ancient despotisms. There is indeed a feeling that the modern dictators display an unhealthy concern with the arts of propaganda without which their regimes would burst asunder from the pressure of internal discord. Dictators are commonly supposed to maintain themselves in power and to protect their regimes against dissension by a policy, in part of brute strength and in part of the "manipulation" of public opinion through propaganda. Studies of the political institutions of the Soviet Union, Nazi Germany and other totalitarian states invariably draw attention to the complex apparatus of official propaganda and censorship, with the implication that the dictators have become skilled professionals in arts that remain relatively underdeveloped in the democracies. The dictators themselves make the same assumptions about their skill as propagandists. Because the concept of a rational, free-willed electorate is at the heart of our democratic ideology we find it comforting to adopt this attitude that the dictators are more dependent on propaganda than we are. We build two contrasting images: one of the sheeplike, unthinking victims of Soviet propaganda, the other of the free, independent spirit of the democracies.

We are often encouraged in this image-making by definitions of propaganda which restrict the terms to the propagation of "controversial," "unaccepted," "dishonest," or "non-rational" ideas and values. The image is further strengthened by a common tendency to identify the dissemination of alien ideas as propaganda, and to reject this term when considering the advocacy of our own faith. The effect, of course, is to make us more aware of, and more receptive to, non-democratic appeals. This is especially true when someone from a democracy, say a tourist or a journalist, visits a totalitarian state. Such a person is extremely sensitive to the existence of authoritarian propaganda, if only because he is a stranger and therefore quick to observe the unfamiliar. The American in Moscow would no doubt note as significant many things which the Muscovite would not even see. The propaganda is seen because it is new to the visitor, and it is seen *as propaganda* because its content is generally unfavorable to the visitor's own beliefs and values. And because the foreign observer in the dictatorship is aware of much more propaganda than he ever noticed at home, he tends to argue that there *is* more, although, in terms of total volume and especially in variety of appeal, there is likely to be less propaganda in a dictatorship than in a democracy of comparable size.

This last statement is made with some reservation for two reasons. First of all, there are as yet no satisfactory techniques for measuring the volume of propaganda. Because there is no such thing as a measurable "unit" of propaganda, there is not even agreement about what it is that should be measured. Whatever the unit of measurement, however, there is obviously an overwhelming flood of propaganda material being disseminated by countless agencies. There are some statistics to support tentative conclusions, but for the most part we must talk in terms of "more or less" or "tendencies and trends." Great precision is not possible, but we can say that in the democracies the general body of citizens are likely to be confronted more often with attempts to influence their political attitudes than are their counterparts in the dictatorships.

Another word of caution may be necessary. The discussion is concerned with actual states with all their imperfections, and not with ideal, perfected democracies. This means that the study of propaganda in a democracy will not be the same thing as the study of democratic propaganda, i.e., propaganda by democrats or for the democratic ideal. Propaganda in a democratic country also includes much propaganda by people and groups who reject, misunderstand, or are ambivalent towards the ideals of democracy.

Although, as already suggested, there are as yet no satisfactory measurement techniques, there are still some reasonably meaningful guides to the volume of propaganda in a society. One such guide is an analysis of the availability of the means of communication. How many people are likely to perceive such propaganda as is disseminated? What contacts are there between the propagandists and their audience? The value of information drawn from this kind of analysis is admittedly limited, but it is not without significance. Consider, for example, the figures on the table on page 138.

There has been no attempt here to "weigh" the propaganda of the various media, to assess the relative propaganda content of, say *Pravda* and the *Chicago Tribune,* or to assign relative importance to such different forms of propaganda as speeches, editorials, cartoons or documentary films. But the figures are extremely interesting. They show that, with very few exceptions, the citizens of the major democracies are exposed to a substantially greater number of potential sources of propaganda than are their counterparts in the Soviet orbit. There may be more political propaganda on the Russian television networks than on the American, but political material is broadcast in both countries and for every Russian who has a television receiver, there are thirty-three viewers in the United States. Within the Soviet Union this imbalance of propaganda media is, however, partially offset by a massive and highly

AVAILABILITY OF COMMUNICATION MEDIA

Country	(A)	(B)	(C)	(D)	(E)
United States of America	337	13,462	12.6	925	293.5
United Kingdom	573	22,143	14.6	285	172.9
Canada	244	1,537	10.7	582	185.4
France	246	11,725	9.7	239	22.4
German Federal Republic	277	19,618	13.8	276	39.6
U.S.S.R.	107	63,641	15.1	163	8.82
Poland	150	6,142	8.2	155	3.0
German Democratic Republic	118	7,101	15.7	310	18.1
Czechoslovakia	181	7,929	13.9	236	24.56

(A) Circulation per 1,000 of Population of Daily General-Interest Newspapers.
(B) Production of Books and Non-Periodical Publications—Total Annual Production.
(C) Annual Cinema Attendances per 1,000 of Population.
(D) Number of Radio Receiving Sets per 1,000 of Population.
(E) Number of Television Receiving Sets per 1,000 of Population.

All figures have been taken from UNESCO publication, "Basic Facts and Figures—International Statistics Relating to Education, Culture and Mass Communication," 1959 Edition. Communist China has not been included as in most cases the statistical information is not available.

organized system of "oral agitation"—propaganda carried out on a person-to-person basis by members of the Communist Party. This is not just voluntary propaganda by dedicated enthusiasts, but a specific obligation, a duty, required of all party members.[2]

Within any democratic state there is an astonishing proliferation of propaganda appeals. Of the many media through which these appeals are made, the most extensively used is the press. Much has been written here and elsewhere about the daily newspaper, from the mass-circulation giant down to the small local paper, in all of which propaganda appears in several guises. Added to these are popular journals such as *Reader's Digest, Saturday Evening Post, Time* and the like, which build up a reading public for their own propaganda and for that of their advertisers, by a slick journalistic style and an emphasis on non-political "entertainment" features. The flood of paper is increased by hundreds of trade papers, house magazines, party papers, special interest journals, broadsheets, newsletters, pamphlets, reports, and circulars, any of which can be used, at least occasionally, as a vehicle for propaganda. Within the United States in 1957 the consumption of newsprint, in terms of kilograms per inhabitant, was 36.3, compared with 20.0 in the United Kingdom and 1.6 in the Soviet Union. This is not a comparison of the volume of propaganda, but simply of the volume of possible opportunities for printed propaganda. One major reason for the difference in the volume of democratic propaganda compared with authoritarian propaganda arises from the fact that within a democracy one has to include not only the official and near-official appeals of the government and the party that controls it, but also the propaganda of rival parties and of numerous and often mutually antagonistic groups such as labor, business, agriculture, churches, racial, cultural and national interests, movements for social-political reform or reaction, political societies, and those ephemeral groups which come into being and fade away again as issues arise and disappear.

A dictatorship, where all propaganda is official propaganda, cannot hope to match this profusion of appeals to public opinion, nor has it any need to do so. Much propaganda in our society is simply counter-propaganda called into existence by the fact of an opposition; an opposition which would not be tolerated in an authoritarian regime. The British Research Defense League, for example, exists to protect medical research against the efforts of the Anti-Vivisection Society, and in the United States the Nation Lawyers Guild was formed to unite lawyers of "New Deal inclinations" against the conservative leanings of the bar associations. A recent publication of the United States Senate listed some three hundred political organizations more or less suspect by the Federal Government.[3] They ranged from the Abraham Lincoln Brigade through the American League Against War and Fascism, the Ku Klux Klan, the National Committee to Win Amnesty for Smith Act Victims, and the Yiddisher Kultur Farband, to the Yugoslav Seaman's Club, Inc. All of these will be engaged, to some degree, in propaganda activities. None, if suspect by the Government, could operate openly in a non-democratic society.

Even in an analysis of the volume of propaganda in favor of the established order, whether disseminated by the government, the government party, or by private interests with a stake in the preservation of the status quo, the balance still seems to be in favor of the democracies. One single, centralized organization, *Agitprop,* the Department of Agitation and Propaganda of the Central Committee of the Communist Party of the Soviet Union, is responsible for all official propaganda activities in the Soviet Union. When such an organization undertakes the strengthening of national patriotism, it cannot hope to challenge, in terms of volume and variety, the total patriotic outpourings of the American parties, the cinema, newspaper and broadcasting industries (even if some of these latter are engaged in propaganda only as an offshoot, an incidental, to moneymaking), and the hundreds of self-styled patriotic groups such as the American First Committee, the Daughters of the American Revolution, and the Committee for Constitutional Government. In the democracies, a great many people, voluntary organizations, and individuals, are engaged in propaganda at every level. No dictatorship can tolerate this vast array of unsupervised activity and none have the resources to compete at the official level. Soviet official propaganda may be more extensive than propaganda by the American government, but it cannot be greater than the total of public and private propaganda within the United States.

PROPAGANDA IN A DICTATORSHIP

It has already been made clear that in a dictatorship the sum total of propaganda influences—the volume of propaganda—is certainly not greater, and is probably significantly less, than in a comparable democracy. There is also a certain amount of evidence that the propaganda of the dictators is often technically weak. Of course, no one questions the skill of the Nazis in drawing the maximum emotional response from the rallies and parades, nor can anyone doubt the pervasive influence of Soviet "personal agitation" tactics. But the full impact of these measures is often undermined by failings, and especially the failing of stolid dullness, in other media.

The fate of the German press illustrates the consequences of a repetitious and unimaginative propaganda. In Germany in 1933, where there was a high level of literacy, there was an extensive and respected press. As soon as the Nazis assumed power they began a policy of suppression of all newspapers and periodicals unsympathetic to the Nazi cause. In 1932, the total number of newspapers and periodicals published in Germany was something over eleven thousand. By 1935, this number had declined to eight thousand five hundred, in spite of the two thousand new journals launched by the Nazis. Not only did the total number of papers decline, a fact easily explained by the program of suppression, but those that survived, even though supported by the regime, suffered a decline in circulation. Fewer people read the Nazi papers after Hitler came into power than in the months immediately before. The greatest single explanation for this decline in newspaper reading is the dullness and uniformity of the press under an authoritarian regime.

Party newspapers and magazines continue to be read by a small number of dedicated supporters of the party—and by a certain number who find it advisable to make public demonstration of their loyalty. But the mass of the citizens quickly become bored with the constant repetition of the same clichés, the same stereotyped images of friends and foes, the unchanging adulation of the party and its inspired leaders. The single-minded dedication of the party fanatic has little appeal to the man in the street, and after a time he ceases to read or listen unless, as in the case of Hitler's broadcasts, a secret police force makes inattention dangerous.

The failure of much of their propaganda to appeal to the people has been recognized in all leading dictatorships, even by such men as Dr. Goebbels, who was undoubtedly the most skilled of all totalitarian propagandists. He acknowledged in his diaries that within Germany his propaganda "didn't seem to have the right spark to it." One of his directives to the press, issued in November, 1939, declared. "In times of strong political tension it was necessary that the press obtain a certain uniformity. But now it must lose no time in making efforts to get out of this monotony." [4] This demand that the press use its initiative and imagination to attract new readers was frequently repeated,[5] but its effect was negated by a series of day-by-day press directives which subjected the whole German press to the most rigid control, even to the extent of specifying headlines and layout.

The Soviet leaders have from time to time shown that they are similarly aware of the shortcomings of their propaganda. In 1957, for example, *Pravda* charged that "Soviet newspapers are insipid, lifeless, deadly dull and difficult to read." The same paper, in May, 1956, demanded a major improvement in the operation of Russian newspapers in general. To quote from its attack—"Such faults as the superficial and insipid manner of describing life in our country, the clichés, the generalizations and the political jargon must be resolutely repressed." [6] It is interesting to note that since 1956, when a campaign against stolid dullness began, a marked improvement has been reported in the character of the Soviet press. Modern techniques of layout and illustration, once condemned by Stalin as signs of bourgeois decadence, have been adopted in a large number of papers. A new paper, *Sovetskaya Rossia,* since it was founded in 1956, has built itself up to be the second largest paper in the country[7] by following the pattern of the Western "popular" press, with an emphasis on local events, sports, theater, film and human interest stories which would not have been tolerated by Stalin.

It is not only the Soviet press that is at fault. Comments on Communist radio broadcasts that appeared in the newspapers of East Berlin during the spring of 1952 indicated that the Communists themselves were beginning to see the weaknesses of their radio propaganda, and to realize that "methodical dogmatism does not draw listeners." A series of articles demanded that *Radio Berlin* show "more sensitivity to what is alive," to use fewer catchwords and to use humor and conversation to establish a more "creative optimism." [8]

The features that reduce the value of the Soviet press and radio propaganda are also to be found in films in which ideological content and educative value are deemed more important criteria than entertainment. For a brief period in the revolutionary era, when dominated by such men as Eisenstein and Pudovkin, the Soviet cinema was imaginative and dynamic. But with the growing insistence on its conformity to a Marxist strait jacket, it stagnated and for years relied on a series of standard situations presented in formal style. The Russian film became almost as ritualistic in plot as Chinese classic drama—and had about as much emotional impact on its Russian audience. The demands for absolute conformity and orthodoxy, characteristic of an authoritarian regime, inhibit a too-imaginative propaganda.

The Closed Society

Despite the inferior quality of much of their propaganda and despite the limitations on the volume of propaganda, the modern dictators have obviously been fairly successful in creating something akin to a mass mind, a controlled disciplined population, a uniform rigidity of mental attitudes. Hitler, Mussolini, Khrushchev, and Mao have apparently been able to mold public opinion far more easily than can any propagandist in our society. There are two reasons for this. The first is the extent to which the techniques of persuasion are supplemented by force and terror. The second is the obvious reason that *Agitprop* and its equivalents tolerate no rivals. There are no groups trying to undo their work or suggesting that it might be done differently. In short, totalitarian propaganda operates within what might be called a closed environment. We should all by now be aware of the determination with which authoritarian governments seek to protect their citizens from the contaminating influences of heresy, doubt and controversy. The government, or the Leader, as sole interpreter of right and wrong, assumes the moral responsibility for preserving the faith of its people. It creates an environment in which none but orthodox thoughts may circulate.

And, of course, the beliefs and values that most of us hold are conditioned by our environment. The decisions we make, by whatever rational or non-rational process, must be based on what we have perceived; and the type of decision we are capable of making must be limited by the sort of evidence available to us. Knowing this, the dictators of today strive to set up a situation where the only values that may be discussed are the values approved by the state, where the stuff of genuine political controversy is carefully screened out. It is not so much the power of positive propaganda that makes loyal Communists and loyal Fascists, but the creation of a closed environment in which no opposing ideas are ever uttered. No one should be surprised by the discovery that great numbers of poorly-educated people in Russia or China are willing and enthusiastic supporters of their governments. They know nothing of any other way of life. The dictators rely less on propaganda than on rigid censorship. Censorship in a dictatorship is not a wartime expedient, nor is it restricted to matters of military security. It is, rather, a continuing and coördinated factor in government policy, a major weapon for the preservation of power and for the maintenance of social control. In a fortress shut off by censorship and defended by secret police, the propagandists of the dictatorships have succeeded in building a *Brave New World* of thought control. We are now familiar with the "closed mind" state of the citizens of modern dictatorships, their near-automatic utterances of the stock reply to every question, the substitution of slogans for thought and the apparent inability to accept even the possibility of error by the leaders. The ability of the party to impose a "true" in contrast to a "heretical" theory of genetics or music, the subordination of scientific or historical facts to the demands of a political philosophy demonstrate the power of the government over the popular mind.

In the philosophy of totalitarianism, such conditioning of the masses in their own interest is accepted as one of the duties of a government which alone knows where that interest really lies. The propaganda of the dictators is not intended to stimulate individual thought; rather it is de-signed, by reinforcing existing prejudices and attitudes, to absolve the individual from the necessity of any thought on political issues. The totalitarian state, as the sole judge of the good of the nation, has authority over every act and thought of every individual and group. All activities, com-mercial, industrial, educational, ethical, intellectual, reli-gious, or leisure, are the concern of the state, which has the "right" and the power to order, to forbid and to regulate. Propaganda and censorship are the weapons of the totali-tarian state, guaranteeing its "absolute control over the spiritual forces of the nation." 9

So much has already been written of totalitarian con-trols over press, film, and radio that a detailed treatment here is quite unnecessary. In Nazi Germany, in Fascist Italy, in the Communist regimes of Russia, China and East Europe, control of the mass media is the exclusive pre-rogative of the state. In Germany, for example, Dr. Goeb-bels was made responsible for controlling the propaganda activities of both Party and State. Within the Party he held the post of Head of the Reich Propaganda Office and within the State he was Minister for People's Enlightenment and Propaganda and also President of the Reich Chamber of Culture. Through these three offices, Goebbels's control over communication was complete. His authority extended even to the manufacture and sale of newsprint, movie cameras, and musical instruments. Without his authority, nothing could legally be performed or displayed in public; nothing could be printed; there could be no speeches or parades. The government took an active part in every form of propaganda and at the same time denied all opposition groups legal access to any means of communication.

With similar thoroughness in the Soviet Union the "printing presses, stocks of paper, public buildings, the streets, means of communication, and other material requisites" for the exercise of the freedoms of speech, press, assembly, mass meeting, street procession, and demonstration are reserved to "the toilers and their organizations," which means, in effect, the Communist party.[10] The principal agency of control is the Department of Agitation and Propaganda of the Party's Central Committee (Agitprop) which performs, with equal efficiency, the functions of the various agencies directed in Germany by Joseph Goebbels.

But the control of mass media, so fully discussed in the literature of totalitarianism, is not by itself sufficient to guarantee the "purity" of the closed society. All contact with alien ideas is suspect and where it cannot be entirely eliminated, it must be zealously supervised. For this reason, during the last years of Stalin's rule, international tourist traffic between East and West was virtually nonexistent. Visitors to the Soviet Union found their movements narrowly circumscribed, as to a lesser degree they still are, and Russians themselves found it inadvisable to speak to foreigners on any but official matters. Russian citizens who left the country on any business found their actions constantly supervised. Even Russian athletic teams at international games lived apart from the competitors of other countries and under the watchful eye of trusted party men. The regime could not permit any unauthorized contact with an alien environment. In the capital cities of the satellite countries even the reading rooms, which had been established by some of the foreign missions, were closed, even though they had been used by only a minute fraction of the population.[11] The Communist or Fascist propagandist thus works under very special conditions. The official propagandist, as the sole legal propagandist, has nothing to fear from internal counter-propaganda. His privileged position is backed by the armed force of police and army. With the state physically and mentally isolated, he can operate, confident that his statements cannot be openly challenged, however much they might be privately questioned. Having little, if anything, to fear from internal opposition, the totalitarian propagandist can concentrate on keeping the society closed, on restricting alien contacts and on rendering harmless such disturbing thoughts as do enter. Within the dictatorship, this isolation is apparently not regarded as intolerable, for the image has been created of a wise, benevolent leadership protecting the people from the corruption of alien, and therefore evil, ideas.

> The cult of hatred and xenophobia is the cheapest and surest method of obtaining from the masses the ignorant and savage patriotism which puts the blame for every political folly or social misfortune upon the foreigner.[12]

Faced with these conditions, the democratic propagandist is at a serious disadvantage in the Cold War. The nature of the democratic society is such that anti-democratic ideas can circulate with relative freedom, but counter-propaganda in the territory of rival powers is exceedingly difficult and costly. There is only one consolation. No society, not even the Soviet Union under Stalin, is completely closed. The development of modern communications and the contacts which must be made between states today, even hostile states, are such that no country can completely exclude foreign ideas. Some concepts of Western democracy, some corrections of false images of the democratic way of life, will circulate within the dictatorship. And because these ideas are forbidden, because they question the orthodox viewpoint, they have the added value of "forbidden pleasures," and for this reason are more widely distributed than they might otherwise be.

FREEDOM OF PROPAGANDA IN
THE DEMOCRATIC SOCIETY

The conclusion now reached is that the undoubtedly greater power of the totalitarian propagandist rests, not on any superiority of technique, but on a monopoly control over the means of propaganda and the forceful exclusion of all rival propaganda. It is the absence of any hostile sentiments, of any doubtings, criticisms, or refutations of his claims, that guarantee his dominating role. In the light of this conclusion it can be argued that in a genuine democracy there will be the greatest possible degree of free competition among the propagandists for various causes. This competition is desirable, not only to prevent the emergence of a totalitarian monopoly, or to weaken the authority of established propagandists, but also because the fillip of new, controversial ideas is in itself a stimulating, educating force in a community that naturally tends to ignorance and apathy in political and social affairs. Rival propaganda campaigns are one of the most important forces for provoking individual thinking on any issue. Now, although a democratic government may give a lead to public opinion and perhaps provide a focus for public discussion, it is not part of its function to determine the religious, philosophic, political, economic, social, or purely eccentric beliefs of its people. The government is not the guardian of the public conscience and has no authority to object to the faith of any of its citizens or to their desire to convert others to that faith.[13] The democratic system is based on the assumption that the electorate is capable of making a rational decision in the selection of policies and governments. The process of democracy could be defined as the evolution of a coherent public opinion by the percolation of individual ideas through the community and the final expression of that public opinion in law. And however much this definition may be qualified by evidence of non-rational motivations, it is still basically valid. Democracy is built on a belief in a people as wise as their governors. To give the government, therefore, authority to protect the people from "undesirable" propaganda would, by implying superior wisdom on the part of the governors, be a denial of democracy.

Against this general argument for a completely "open" society in the field of propaganda, the view is often expressed that any extension of propaganda will result in a further lowering of the moral tone of all propaganda, and that, in the struggle to gain precedence in a competitive world, the propagandists will resort to increasingly emotional and non-rational techniques to the detriment of an intelligent public opinion. This argument is supported by reference to examples of highly colored, one-sided appeals to the emotions, examples that abound in our present society.

Yet this evidence is misleading. During the past fifty years, there has been an enormous increase in the volume of propaganda disseminated in all the Western democracies. Radio, television, and the cinema were all unknown forces at the beginning of the century, while today more people read more newspapers, books, and periodicals than ever before. But although there has been a substantial increase in the volume of propaganda, and although most propaganda is still highly emotional in content, there is no evidence that the propaganda of today is any lower in its moral or intellectual level than it was fifty or more years ago. To see this one has only to compare the descriptions of electoral behavior in the late nineteenth century with those of present decades.[14]

The conclusion that must be drawn from any such comparison is that the level of political maturity and sophistication in the major Western democracies is higher now than at any time in the past and that it is continuing to rise. There are many explanations for this, including the sobering influence of two world wars and the fear of a third, the changing structure and character of the party system, legislation against bribery and corruption, the relative increase in the importance of national and international issues over purely local matters and, perhaps most important, a changing social structure that provides a healthier environment for individual reflective thought.[15] Human nature may still be largely irrational, the electorate may still respond more readily to emotional appeals, but there is no evidence that an increase in the volume of propaganda has led to an increase in irrationalism. Actually it seems that the reverse is the case and that the electorate of today, better educated than in the past, is increasingly prepared to listen and respond to appeals to reason.

It is not claimed that all modern propaganda displays reasoned objectivity, but it is claimed that an enormous increase in the volume of propaganda is not necessarily followed by any significant lowering of its rational content. Once this can be accepted, the true function of propaganda in a democratic society is more easily understood. The present position in all modern democracies is that people who are uninterested and poorly informed on political and social questions are periodically asked to give their verdict on the way these things have been conducted. The politically interested spend a great deal of energy and money in making sure that the greatest possible number do, in fact, give their verdict, irrespective of their knowledge of the issues at stake. It should be obvious that this system will not work as it should unless most of those who vote do so because they are concerned about the results and are informed on the issues. But, within the modern democratic state, the bulk of the population is, for much of the time, not interested in political questions. Many citizens are poorly informed about political matters and lack both the intellectual ability and the interest necessary to acquire further knowledge. Politicians and political scientists who assume that because they are personally interested in politics, it is so with all men, forget that other people have many competing claims upon their attention. They have, first of all, to earn a living and for many this is a full-time, dispiriting drudgery that leaves little energy or enthusiasm for further social activity. Then there are the many and varied counter-demands on leisure time. Because they lack the time and the interest, the majority of people if left to themselves will just not bother with politics, except perhaps for a few minutes on voting day. A fairly widespread apathy towards social and political questions is generally accepted as one of the unalterable facts of our present society.

If a democracy is to succeed, there must be a fairly intelligent participation in politics by a substantial section of the community. The majority of people cannot, therefore, be left to themselves. The apathetic must be aroused from their apathy and encouraged to interest themselves in political controversy. This is the first task of the propagandist, to stimulate an interested public discussion, to present the material of political debate in a manner that will invite wide popular participation. Unlike Hitler, the democratic leader cannot compel people to listen to his propaganda, but he must present it in a form that will attract their interest. This means that anyone seeking popular support in a democracy must make some concessions to existing standards of education and must acknowledge the force of the non-rational in human behavior. To a very large extent, then, a truly "public" opinion is possible only when the leaders of society make use of such propaganda techniques as slogans, parades, appeals to prejudice and sentiment, and high pressure publicity. Even the most sophisticated societies must use symbols such as crown or flag for abstract ideas like the nation.

It is true that in some cases propaganda may dull the capacity for critical thinking. Certain forms of war propaganda, reinforced by censorship and the natural wartime decline in toleration, were designed to create a state of mass hysteria and unrestrained patriotism in which rational thought would be impossible. But not all propaganda is like this. The term embraces many activities that stimulate, rather than dull, individual critical thinking, that vitalize public opinion by bringing to its notice, in a form that attracts attention, the issues of domestic and foreign politics. Instead of condemning party propagandists as perverters of the democratic system, we should encourage them to develop even further their machinery for passing on the material, that is, the facts and the interpretations of facts which form the basis of political discussion.

However, while the existing facts of human behavior and the political world make some recourse to emotional propaganda necessary, the basic ideals to which the democrat owes allegiance make it impossible for him to make use of any and every propaganda tactic. Although he may color his material to give it a more popular appeal and to make it stand out in a competitive background, and although he may use flags, parades and bands, slogans, and so on, to present abstract ideas and complex policies, he cannot adopt practices that would make a complete mockery of his professed belief in the worth of human dignity. He must eschew tactics which would go beyond mere recognition of existing human weaknesses, which would tend to the further debasement of political morality. This moral limitation on the propaganda techniques available to the democrat is of fundamental importance in separating a democratic from a non-democratic approach to the use of propaganda.[16]

CONCLUSION

From this study of propaganda as it is used and controlled in both democratic and non-democratic societies in peace and in war, one may conclude that the effect of propaganda in a dictatorship is quite different from its effect in a democracy. Within a dictatorship we find an environment, established through censorship and physical repression, that is favorable to the development of attitudes of unity, orthodoxy and conformity. The role of propaganda here is largely one of confirming and giving official recognition to these attitudes, established originally by the environment. Propaganda may have some importance in strengthening attitudes, bringing waverers back into the fold, reviving flagging enthusiasms, bringing official views to the notice of the apathetic and the uninterested, announcing changes in the details of basic policy, highlighting certain effects from time to time, and so on, but the principal effect is that of confirming people in the "rightness" of their already firmly-held beliefs.

Within a democracy the average propagandist probably still has ambitions of molding a public mind to his own design, but the result of his propaganda is somewhat different. The actual effect of propaganda in a democratic society is to present to the public certain material, facts, opinions, misrepresentations, ideas, or anything else, in such a manner that it can be seen in highly competitive surroundings and then, having been seen, can be understood and perhaps acted upon. There is at the present time some evidence to suggest that the way it is acted upon is not always the way the propagandist hoped it would be, that the public make their own individual decisions about the propaganda before them.[17] This does not mean that it will always be a wise or rational decision; it might be based on all manner of prejudices, habits, non-rational impulses, or instincts, but at least it is a decision made by the individual and not by the propagandist. The propaganda makes the people aware of the issues to be considered, but it seems to have less effect than once imagined in determining how people will react to these issues. In short, then, in a democracy the effect of propaganda is largely to provide the material for the creation of public opinion.

Official propaganda within the modern dictatorships, less effective than the voluntary propaganda of a free society and more limited in volume than the total of propaganda appeals in a democracy, serves largely to confirm and strengthen attitudes created by a closed environment. Within the democracies the actual effect of propaganda is to provide the stuff of political argument: the material for the formation of public opinion. The danger in our society is not that public opinion will be degraded by too much propaganda, but that, without the stimulating effect of genuinely rival propagandas, there might be established something approaching the closed society in which despotism flourishes.

NOTES

~~~~~~~~~~~~~~~~~~~~~~~~~~~~~~~~~~~~~~~

INTRODUCTION

1. B. L. Smith, "The Political Communication Specialist in Our Times," in B. L. Smith, *et al., Propaganda, Communication and Public Opinion* (Princeton University Press, 1946), p. 31.
2. A. Hitler, Mein Kampf (Chamberlain translation; New York: Reynal & Hitchcock, 1939) pp. 714-15—A comment on the Treaty of Versailles.

CHAPTER ONE   The Theory of Propaganda

1. For a full historical and descriptive treatment of the papal Propaganda see U. Benigni, "Propaganda," *Catholic Encyclopaedia*, XII (1911), pp. 456-61.
2. W. T. Brande, "Propaganda," *Dictionary of Science, Literature and Art* (London, 1842).
3. R. J. R. G. Wreford, "Propaganda, Evil and Good," *The Nineteenth Century and After*, XCIII (1923), pp. 514-24.
4. H. D. Lasswell, "The Theory of Political Propaganda," *American Political Science Review*, XXI (1927), p. 627.
5. *Ibid.*
6. H. D. Lasswell and D. Blumenstock, *World Revolutionary Propaganda* (New York: Alfred A. Knopf, 1939), p. 9.
7. This thesis is put forward in *World Revolutionary Propaganda* (1939) and in the Introduction to *Propaganda and Promotional Activities* (1935).
8. L. W. Doob, *Propaganda, Its Psychology and Technique* (New York: Henry Holt, 1935), pp. 29-35.
9. *Ibid.* pp. 51-2.
10. *Ibid.* p. 54. See also Graham Wallas' treatment of "suggestion" in Chapter Two.
11. *Ibid.* pp. 75-6 and 89.
12. *Ibid.* p. 80.
13. L. W. Doob, *Public Opinion and Propaganda* (London: Cresset, 1949), especially Chap. xi.
14. *Ibid.* p. 237.
15. *Ibid.* p. 240.
16. R. E. Summers (ed.), *America's Weapons of Psycho-

logical Warfare, [The Reference Shelf 23 (4)], (New York: Wilson, 1951), p. 39.

17. A survey of several classifications was made by C. H. Wooddy in "Propaganda and Education" in *The Annals of the American Academy of Political and Social Science,* CLXXIX (1935), pp. 227-39. Some of these are discussed in the pages that follow.
18. *Ibid.* p. 227.
19. *Ibid.* p. 228.
20. *Ibid.* p. 231.
21. J. Bryce, *Modern Democracies* (New York: Macmillan, 1921), II, p. 505.
22. W. S. Churchill, *Their Finest Hour* (Boston: Houghton Mifflin, 1949), p. 339.
23. F. E. Lumley, "The Nature of Propaganda," *Sociology and Social Research,* XIII (1929), pp. 315-24.
24. Published 1933.
25. F. E. Lumley, *The Propaganda Menace* (New York: Century, 1933), p. 44.

CHAPTER TWO　The Development of Propaganda

1. A. de Tocqueville, *Democracy in America* (World's Classics Ed., Oxford University Press, 1945), pp. 297-98.
2. *Ibid.* p. 192.
3. W. McDougall, *An Introduction to Social Psychology* (1908); G. Wallas, *Human Nature in Politics* (1908), and *The Great Society* (1914); W. Lippmann, *A Preface to Politics* (1913), and *Public Opinion* (1922); and W. Trotter, *Instincts of the Herd in Peace and War* (1916).
4. G. Wallas, *The Great Society* (New York: Macmillan, 1914), p. 128.
5. W. Trotter, *Instincts of the Herd in Peace and War* (London: Fisher Unwin, 1916). Trotter clearly owes much to Le Bon's study, *The Crowd.*
6. Trotter, *op. cit.* pp. 216-19. See also G. Mosca, *Elementi di Scienza Politica* (Italy, 1896). English translation, *The Ruling Class* is by H. D. Kahn (New York: McGraw-Hill, 1939).
7. See W. Bagehot, *The English Constitution* (Second Edition; 1872), where he writes: "No one will contend that the ordinary working man who has no special skill, and who is only rated because he has a house, can judge much of intellectual matters." p. 15.
8. See Wallas, *The Great Society,* for a discussion along similar lines.
9. D. Thomson, *England in the Nineteenth Century,* (Penguin Books, 1950), p. 42.

10. H. Heaton, *Economic History of Europe* (New York: Harper & Bros., 1936), p. 553.
11. See, in particular, F. L. Mott, *American Journalism* (New York, 1941) and S. Morison, *The English Newspaper* (Cambridge, 1932).
12. UNESCO, *Basic Facts and Figures 1959.*
13. A detailed history of advertising would be out of place here. The reader is referred to H. Simpson, *A History of Advertising from the Earliest Times* or G. B. Hotchkiss, *An Outline of Advertising.*
14. See, for example, W. D. Scott, "The Psychology of Advertising," *Atlantic Monthly,* XCIII (1904), pp. 29-36.
15. R. S. Lambert, *Propaganda* (London: Nelson, 1938), p. 32.
16. W. Albig, *Modern Public Opinion* (New York: McGraw-Hill, 1956), p. 285.
17. H. C. Brown, "Advertising and Propaganda," *International Journal of Ethics,* XL (1929), pp. 39-40.
18. B. Jerrold, "On the Manufacture of Public Opinion," *Nineteenth Century,* XIII (1883), pp. 1080-92.
19. S. Kydd, *A Sketch on the Growth of Public Opinion* (London, 1888), p. 84.
20. In *Human Nature in Politics.* The page references in the following two paragraphs are from the first edition (1908).
21. The quotations in this paragraph are from *Public Opinion,* pp. 248-49.
22. Any epistemologists who object to the use of the phrase "genuine knowledge" are referred to Lippmann. A fuller treatment of the topic here would be an unwarranted digression.
23. G. Sorel, *Reflection on Violence* (London: Allen and Unwin, 1915), pp. 135 *ff.*
24. B. Mussolini in a speech in Naples in 1922, quoted by H. Finer, *Mussolini's Italy* (New York: Henry Holt, 1935), p. 218.

CHAPTER THREE   Propaganda at War

1. B. Russell, *Power—A New Social Analysis* (London: Allen and Unwin, 1938), p. 135.
2. H. W. Steed, *Through Thirty Years* (London: Heinemann, 1924). See especially Chap. xv in Vol. II.
3. L. Farago, in *German Psychological Warfare* (New York: Committee for National Morale, 1941) has questioned the value of German propaganda efforts in this field. There was, however, an attempt to inculcate a militant attitude and Moysset's general argument is still valid.

4. All quotations in the preceding three paragraphs are from Steed, *op. cit.,* pp. 192-94.

5. H. Lasswell, *Propaganda Technique in the World War* (New York: Peter Smith, 1927), pp. 216-17.

6. "We can surely congratulate ourselves that our enemies have no Wilson Fourteen Points." Goebbels's Diary for January 25, 1942, as quoted by L. P. Lochner, *The Goebbels Diaries* (New York: Doubleday, 1948), p. 47.

7. C. Stuart, *Secrets of Crewe House* (London: Hodder and Stoughton, 1920), p. 2.

8. H. W. Steed, *op. cit.,* II, p. 226.

9. *The Times History of the War* (London, 1919), XXI, p. 133.

10. G. Creel, *How We Advertised America* (New York: Harper & Bros., 1920), pp. 13-14.

11. C. E. Merriam, "American Publicity in Italy," *American Political Science Review,* XIII (1919), p. 554.

12. D. Brownrigg, *Indiscretions of the Naval Censor* (London: Cassell, 1920).

13. *Ibid.* p. 33.

14. From the Introduction to his *Falsehood in Wartime* (London: Allen and Unwin, 1928).

15. M. Garnett, "Propaganda," *Contemporary Review,* CXLVII (1935), p. 574.

16. G. G. Bruntz, *Allied Propaganda and the Collapse of the German Empire in 1918* (Stanford University Press, 1938), p. 63.

17. H. Lasswell, *Propaganda Technique in the World War,* p. 206.

18. Composed by Henri Lavedan. The English translation appeared first in John Buchan, *History of the War,* III, pp. 116-17 and was quoted again by Lasswell, *op. cit.,* p. 57.

19. Many instances of false atrocity stories can be found in the books of Ponsonby, Bruntz and Lasswell that have already been mentioned, and also in J. M. Read, *Atrocity Propaganda 1914-1919* (Yale University Press, 1941).

20. A. Ponsonby, *Falsehood in Wartime,* p. 67.

21. *Ibid.,* The same story is reported by Lasswell, *op. cit.,* p. 207.

22. See J. M. Read, *op. cit.,* esp. pp. 6-7, for some evidence of this.

23. J. M. Read, in "Atrocity Propaganda in the Irish Rebellion," *Public Opinion Quarterly,* II (1938), pp. 229-44 has some interesting comments on this theme.

24. In *Propaganda Technique in the World War.*

25. See also L. W. Doob, *Propaganda: Its Psychology and Technique* (New York: Henry Holt, 1935), pp. 306-7.

CHAPTER FOUR   The Techniques of Propaganda

1. M. Ostrogorski, *Democracy and the Organization of Political Parties* (New York: Macmillan, 1908), II, p. 334.
2. G. Mosca, *The Ruling Class* (English Edition; New York; McGraw-Hill, 1939), p. 176. Reprinted by permission.
3. The question of emotional transfer is more fully treated by R. Dodge, "Psychology of Propaganda," *Religious Education,* XV (1920), pp. 241-52.
4. For some illuminating examples of the failure to communicate see M. F. Herz, "Some Psychological Lessons from Leaflet Propaganda in World War II," *Public Opinion Quarterly,* XIII (1949), pp. 471-86.
5. This slogan is, I regret, not original, but I have long forgotten the source.
6. C. Saerchinger, "Radio as a Political Instrument," *Foreign Affairs,* XVI (1938), p. 251.
7. B. Russell, *Free Thought and Official Propaganda* (London: Watts, 1922), pp. 33-40.
8. *Constitution of the U.S.S.R.* Art. 125.
9. T. O. Beachcroft, *British Broadcasting* (London: Longman, 1948), p. 20.
10. U. S. State Department, Office of International Information and Education Exchange, *The World Audience for the Voice of America* (1950), pp. 2-9.
11. H. Cantril and G. W. Allport, *The Psychology of Radio* (New York: Harper & Bros. 1935), p. 20.
12. C. J. Rolo, *Radio Goes to War* (New York: G. P. Putnam, 1940), p. 11.
13. See, for example, W. Scramm (ed.), *The Process and Effects of Mass Communication* (University of Illinois Press, 1935), pp. 80-1.
14. The general headings that follow were suggested by W. Albig's *Modern Public Opinion* (New York: McGraw-Hill, 1956), pp. 463-67.
15. J. S. Mill, *Essay on Liberty* (Everyman Edition; 1948), p. 130.
16. W. Albig, *op. cit.,* p. 482. Reprinted by permission.
17. For a fuller treatment of this theme see G. Allport and L. Postman, "The Basic Psychology of Rumour," in W. Scramm (ed.), *The Process and Effects of Mass Communication,* pp. 141-55.
18. See Allport and Postman, *op. cit.,* and R. H. Knapp, "A Psychology of Rumour," *Public Opinion Quarterly,* VIII (1949), pp. 22-37.
19. A. Campbell and C. A. Metzner, "Books, Libraries and Other Media of Communication," in D. Katz *et al.* (eds.),

Public Opinion and Propaganda (New York: Dryden, 1954), p. 235.

20. Currently there are approximately 15,000 new titles published each year in the United States and about 22,000 in Great Britain.
21. See, for example, B. Berelson, "What Missing the Newspaper Means," in Lazarsfeld and Stanton (eds.), *Communications Research 1948-49* (New York: Harper & Bros., 1949), pp. 111-29.
22. The manner and extent to which public relations men rely on the press is discussed at length by C. S. Steinberg in *The Mass Communicators* (New York: Harper & Bros., 1958).
23. Quoted by F. Hardy in *Grierson on Documentary* (London: Collins, 1946), p. 13.
24. For a fuller treatment of this theme see E. S. Bogardus, *The Making of Public Opinion* (New York: Association Press, 1951), p. 68.
25. L. C. Rosten, *Hollywood* (New York: Harcourt Brace, 1941), p. 359.
26. B. Schulberg, "Movies in America: Fifty Years After," *Atlantic Monthly,* November, 1947, p. 116.
27. Quoted by R. Manvell, *Film* (Penguin Books, 1946), pp. 172-73.
28. L. C. Rosten, "Movies and Propaganda," *Annals of the American Academy of Political and Social Science,* CCLIV (1947), p. 121.
29. *Komsomolskaya Pravda,* December, 1950.
30. Quoted in Manvell and Fraenkel, *Doctor Goebbels, His Life and Death* (London: Heinemann, 1960), p. 187.
31. See J. A. Leith, "The Idea of Art as Propaganda During the French Revolution," Canadian Historical Association Reports (1959), pp. 30-43 and A. L. Herstand, "Art and the Artist in Communist China," *College Art Journal,* XIX (1959).
32. *Cominform Journal* (May, 1951), quoted by H. Hodgkinson, *Doubletalk, the Langauge of Communism* (London: Allen and Unwin, 1955), p. 15.

CHAPTER FIVE Psychological Warfare

1. F. Bertkau and H. Franke, "Geistiger Krieg," (1938), quoted by L. Farago, *German Psychological Warfare* (New York: Committee for National Morale, 1941), p. 142.
2. See P. M. Linebarger, *Psychological Warfare* (New York: Duell, Sloan & Pearce, 1954), pp. 99-101, for a more detailed treatment of the qualifications for psychological warfare.

3. See F. C. Barghoorn, *The Soviet Image of the United States* (New York: Harcourt, Brace, 1950), pp. 21 *ff*.
4. Preface to H. Hodgkinson, *Doubletalk: The Language of Communism* (London: Allen and Unwin, 1955), p. v. See also S. T. Possony's evidence before the House Committee on Un-American Activities, published under the title, *Language as a Communist Weapon* (March, 1959). This contains a valuable discussion of the roots of Communist semantics.
5. H. McClosky and J. E. Turner, *The Soviet Dictatorship*, (New York: McGraw-Hill, 1960), pp. 542-43.
6. See *Resolutions of the Seventh Congress of the Communist International* (New York, 1935).
7. E. Stern-Rubarth, *Propaganda als politisches Instrument* (Berlin, 1921).
8. A. Hitler, *Mein Kampf* (English translation; New York; Reynal & Hitchcock, 1939), p. 234.
9. Manvell and Fraenkel, *Doctor Goebbels, His Life and Death* (London: Heinemann, 1960), p. 90.
10. *Ibid.* pp. 80-1.
11. S. Chakotin, *The Rape of the Masses* (London: Labour Book Service, 1940), p. 84.
12. From a handbill issued by the Nazi party in November, 1933. Cited by F. M. Marx, "State Propaganda in Germany," from H. C. Childs (ed.), *Propaganda and Dictatorship* (Princeton University Press, 1936), p. 17.
13. Quoted in A. H. Chisholm, *The Incredible Years* (New Zealand: Oswald-Sealey, 1944), p. 146.
14. PWE/OWI, *Standing Directive for Psychological Warfare Against Members of the German Armed Forces,* issued in conjunction with the Psychological Warfare Division of SHAEF., June 1944. Reprinted in D. Lerner, *Sykewar* (New York: Stewart, 1949), pp. 403-17.
15. See E. W. Barrett, *Truth is Our Weapon* (New York; Funk & Wagnalls, 1953), p. 39, for comments on this theme.
16. Goebbels's diary entry for May 11, 1942, quoted in L. P. Lochner, *The Goebbels Diaries,* p. 211.
17. Leaflet ZG82, reproduced in L. J. Margolin, *Paper Bullets* (New York; Froben Press, 1946), p. 17.
18. Goebbel's diary entry for March 2, 1942, quoted in L. P. Lochner, *op. cit.,* p. 108.
19. Goebbels's diary entry for March 9, 1943. L. P. Lochner, *op. cit.,* p. 284.
20. E. W. Barrett, *op. cit.,* p. 302.
21. See W. Lippmann, *Public Opinion* (New York: Harcourt, Brace, 1922), Chap. ii.

22. Broadcast from SHAEF. Radio, May 19, 1944. Quoted in D. Lerner, *Sykewar*, pp. 425-26.
23. L. J. Margolin, *Paper Bullets* (New York: Froben, 1946), pp. 121-26.
24. Goebbels's diary entry for November 24, 1943. L. P. Lochner, *op. cit.*, p. 524.
25. Letter of August 12, 1940. W. S. Churchill, *Their Finest Hour* (Boston: Houghton Mifflin, 1949), p. 644.
26. Letter of March 21, 1941, to Minister of Food. W. S. Churchill, *The Grand Alliance* (Boston; Houghton Mifflin, 1950), p. 747. The reference is to proposals for food service for those whose homes have been bombed.
27. The Office of War Information (OWI) ceased independent existence at the end of August, 1945, although it continued to function in a limited way under the control of the State Department. The companion organization, Office of Strategic Services (OSS) was broken up by an Executive Order of September 20, 1945.
28. United States, Office of the Federal Register, *United States Government Organization Manual*, 1960-61, p. 519.
29. *Ibid.*
30. Cited by M. F. Herz, "Some Psychological Lessons from Leaflet Propaganda in World War II," *Public Opinion Quarterly*, XII (1949), p. 472.
31. M. F. Herz, *op. cit.*, p. 475.
32. See E. W. Barrett, *Truth is Our Weapon* (New York: Funk & Wagnalls, 1953), p. 189, for a discussion of these assumptions of Soviet policy.
33. B. W. Patch, "Non-Military Weapons in Cold War Offensive," in R. E. Summers (ed.), *America's Weapons of Psychological Warfare* [Reference Shelf 23 (4)] (New York: Wilson, 1951), p. 32.
34. From a pamphlet, *A Fresh Look at Liberation*, issued by the Committee in 1957.
35. *Ibid.*
36. P. M. Linebarger, *Psychological Warfare* (New York: Duell, Sloan, & Pearce, 1954), pp. 273-74.
37. In *The Rape of the Masses* (London: Labour Book Service, 1940), S. Chakotin devotes a whole chapter to the relation between conditioned reflexes and propaganda.
38. United States Congress, House of Representatives, Committee on Un-American Activities, *Communist Psychological Warfare, (Brainwashing)*, Consultation with Edward Hunter, March 13, 1958, p. 15.
39. *N. Y. Times*, January 6, 1957.
40. United States Congress, *Communist Psychological Warfare, (Brainwashing)*, p. 17.

41. *Ibid.*
42. W. Albig, *Modern Public Opinion* (New York: McGraw-Hill, 1936), p. 307.
43. *Daily Express,* November 14, 1950.

CHAPTER SIX   Propaganda in Two Societies

1. See Chapter Two.
2. The 1952 *Statutes of the Communist Party of the Soviet Union* Sec. 3 (d), provides that it is the duty of the Party member, "Day in and day out to strengthen contact with the masses, to respond promptly to the desires and needs of the working people, and to explain to the non-Party masses the meaning of the Party policy and decisions, mindful that the strength and invincibility of our Party lie in close, inseparable ties with the people."
3. United States Senate, Committee on the Judiciary, *The Technique of Soviet Propaganda,* Appendix, "Organizations Designated Under Executive Order No. 10450." It is stated that, "Membership in or affiliation with a designated organization is one factor to be considered in connection with the employment or retention in employment of individuals in Federal Service."
4. W. Hagemann, *Publizistik im Dritten Reich* (Hamburg, 1948), p. 153, quoted in E. Bramsted, "Joseph Goebbels and National Socialist Propaganda," *Australian Outlook,* VIII (1954), p. 82.
5. See also F. L. Schuman, *The Nazi Dictatorship* (New York: Alfred Knopf, 1939), p. 307.
6. Both quotations from *Pravda* have been taken from the International Press Institute Survey, *The Press in Authoritarian Countries* (Zurich, 1959), p. 16.
7. International Press Institute, *The Press in Authoritarian Countries,* p. 20.
8. See R. K. White, "The New Resistance to International Propaganda," *Public Opinion Quarterly,* XVI (1952), pp. 539-51. White makes the very valid comment that "The psychological resistances of a skeptical, propaganda-weary world must be respected and intelligently taken into account; they cannot simply be battered down."—p. 539.
9. E. Hadamovsky, *Propaganda und Nationale Macht,* quoted by L. Farago, *German Psychological Warfare* (New York: Committee for National Morale, 1941), p. 158.
10. Art. 125 of the *Constitution of the U.S.S.R.* (1936).
11. E. Taborsky, *Conformity Under Communism; a Study of Indoctrination Techniques in East Europe* (Washington: Public Affairs Press, 1958), p. 5.

12. L. Woolf, *Principia Politica* (London: Hogarth, 1953), p. 313.
13. For an article on this general theme, see F. L. Cobb, "The Press and Public Opinion," *The New Republic* (December 31, 1919), pp. 144-47.
14. Using British examples it is interesting to compare, on the one hand, J. Grego, *A History of Parliamentary Elections and Electioneering in the Old Days* (London, 1886) and N. Gash, *Politics in the Age of Peel* (London, 1953) with, on the other hand, D. E. Butler's two books, *The British General Election of 1951* (London, 1952) and *The British General Election of 1955* (London, 1955).
15. The relevance of a healthy physical environment to mature political activity is discussed at length by Graham Wallas in *The Great Society* (New York: Macmillan, 1914).
16. On this general theme see S. Chakotin, *The Rape of the Masses* (London: Labour Book Service, 1940), p. 278 and F. Neumann, *Behemoth—the Structure and Practice of National Socialism* (New York: Oxford University of Press, 1942), p. 357.
17. See T. H. Qualter, "The Manipulation of Popular Impulse," *Canadian Journal of Economics and Political Science,* XXV (1959), for a brief survey of literature on the effectiveness of propaganda in a free society.

A GUIDE TO FURTHER READING

~~~~~~

There is an extensive literature on every aspect of propaganda and public opinion control. The selection of titles listed below will serve to introduce the reader to this literature.

ALBIG, WILLIAM. *Modern Public Opinion.* New York: McGraw-Hill, 1956, 518 pp.

BARGHOORN, F. C. *The Soviet Image of the United States: A Study in Distortion.* New York: Harcourt, Brace, 1950, 297 pp.

BARRETT, E. W. *Truth is Our Weapon.* New York: Funk & Wagnalls, 1953, 355 pp.

BERELSON, BERNARD and JANOWITZ, M. (eds.). *Reader in Public Opinion and Communication* (Enlarged Edition). Glencoe, Illinois: The Free Press, 1953, 611 pp. Reprints over fifty papers, some of them otherwise difficult to acquire.

BRAMSTED, E. "Joseph Goebbels and National Socialist Propaganda 1926-1939: Some Aspects," *Australian Outlook*, VIII (1954), pp. 65-93.

BROWN, H. C. "Advertising and Propaganda: A Study in the Ethics of Social Control," *International Journal of Ethics*, XL (1929), pp. 39-55.

BROWNRIGG, D. E. R. *Indiscrections of the Naval Censor.* London and New York: Cassell, 1920, 279 pp.

BRUNTZ, G. G. *Allied Propaganda and the Collapse of the German Empire in 1918.* Stanford, California: Stanford University Press, 1938, 246 pp.

CANTRIL, HADLEY and ALLPORT, G. W. *The Psychology of Radio.* New York: Harper & Bros., 1935, 276 pp. Comments on the effects of radio in inducing social conformity.

CARR, E. H. *The Twenty Years' Crisis, 1919-1939.* London: Macmillan, 1946. See especially pp. 132-145, "Power Over Opinion."

CHAFEE, ZECHARIAH. *Government and Mass Communications.* (Two volumes). Chicago, Illinois: University Press, 1947, 830 pp. A Report from the Commission on Freedom of the Press.

CHAKOTIN, SERGE. *The Rape of the Masses: The Psychology of Totalitarian Political Propaganda.* London: The Labour Book Service, 1940.

CHILDS, H. C. (ed.). "Pressure Groups and Propaganda," *The Annals of the American Academy of Political and Social Science*, CLXXIX, 1935, 239 pp.

———. *Propaganda and Dictatorship*. Princeton, New Jersey: University Press, 1936, 153 pp. A collection of papers on propaganda in various authoritarian countries.

CREEL, GEORGE. *How We Advertised America: The First Telling of the Amazing Story of the Committee on Public Information that Carried the Gospel of Americanism to Every Corner of the Globe*. New York: Harper & Bros., 1920, 466 pp.

CROSSMAN, R. H. S. *The God That Failed*. New York: Harper & Bros. 1950, 273 pp.

DODGE, R. "Psychology of Propaganda," *Religious Education*, XV (1920), pp. 241-252.

DOOB, L. W. *Propaganda, Its Psychology and Technique*. New York: Henry Holt, 1935, 424 pp.

———. *Public Opinion and Propaganda*. London: Cresset Press, 1949, 600 pp.

FARAGO, LADISLAS (ed.). *German Psychological Warfare*. New York: Committee for National Morale, 1941, 302 pp., including annotated bibliography of 560 entries.

FINER, HERMAN. *Mussolini's Italy*. New York: Henry Holt, 1935, 218 pp. See especially Chaps. vii and viii, which deal with the Fascist propaganda organization.

GEORGE, A. L. *Propaganda Analysis, A Study of Inferences Made from Nazi Propaganda in World War II*. Evanston, Illinois: Row Peterson & Co., 1959, 287 pp.

HERSTAND, A. L. "Art and the Artist in Communist China," *College Art Journal*, XIX, 1959.

HERZ, M. F. "Some Psychological Lessons from Leaflet Propaganda in World War II," *Public Opinion Quarterly*, XII (1949), pp. 471-486.

HITLER, ADOLF. *Mein Kampf*. Translated and annotated by John Chamberlain *et al*. New York: Reynal & Hitchcock, 1939, 1003 pp.

HODGKINSON, HARRY. *Doubletalk: The Language of Communism*. London: Allen and Unwin, 1955, 149 pp. The semantics of psychological warfare.

HOVLAND, C. I. *et al*. *Experiments on Mass Communication*. (Vol. III of Social Science Research Council *Studies in Social Psychology in World War II*). Princeton, New Jersey: University Press, 1949, 343 pp. A thoroughly documented study on the circumstances in which a propaganda campaign failed to achieve its objective.

INTERNATIONAL PRESS INSTITUTE. *Government Pressures on the Press*. I. P. I. Survey No. 4, Zurich, 1955, 130 pp.

————. *The Press in Authoritarian Countries.* I. P. I. Survey No. 5, Zurich, 1959, 201 pp.

KATZ, DANIEL, *et al.*, (eds.). *Public Opinion and Propaganda— A Book of Readings Edited for the Society for the Psychological Study of Social Issues.* New York: Dryden Press, 1954, 779 pp.

KNAPP, R. H. "A Psychology of Rumour," *Public Opinion Quarterly*, VIII (1949), pp. 22-37.

LAMBERT, R. S. *Propaganda.* London: Nelson, 1938, 162 pp.

LASSWELL, H. D. "Propaganda," *Encyclopaedia of the Social Sciences* (1934), XII, pp. 521-527.

————. *Propaganda Technique in the World War*, New York: Peter Smith, 1927, 233 pp.

————. "The Theory of Political Propaganda," *American Political Science Review*, XXI (1927), pp. 627-631.

LASSWELL, H. D. and BLUMENSTOCK D. *World Revolutionary Propaganda—A Chicago Study.* New York: Alfred A. Knopf, 1939, 393 pp.

LASSWELL, H. D., CASEY, R. D. and SMITH B. L. *Propaganda and Promotional Activities, An Annotated Bibliography.* Minneapolis, Minnesota: University of Minesota Press, 1935, 450 pp.

LAVINE, HAROLD and WECHSLER, JAMES. *War Propaganda and the United States.* (Published for the Institute of Propaganda Analysis). New Haven, Connecticut: Yale University Press, 1940, 363 pp.

LENIN, V. I. "Where to Begin" (1910), (*Selected Works* Vol. II, pp. 15-23). Translated by the Marx-Engels-Lenin Institute, Moscow. New York: International Publishers, 1934.

LERNER, DANIEL. *Sykewar: Psychological Warfare Against Germany: D-Day to VE-Day.* New York: G. W. Stewart, 1949, 463 pp. A Detailed study of the Psychological Warfare Division of SHAEF.

LINEBARGER, P. M. *Psychological Warfare.* (Second edition). New York: Duell, Sloan & Pearce, 1954, 318 pp.

LIPPMANN, WALTER *Public Opinion.* New York: Harcourt, Brace, 1922, 427 pp. See especially Part III which deals with Lippmann's theory of stereotypes, pp. 79-158.

LOCHNER, L. P. *The Goebbels Diaries, 1942-43.* Edited and translated by the author. New York: Doubleday, 1948, 547 pp. Annotated extracts from the diaries of Dr. Goebbels during this critical period of the war.

LUMLEY, F. E. *The Propaganda Menace.* New York and London: Century, 1933, 454 pp.

LUTZ, R. H. *The Causes of the German Collapse in 1918.* Sections of the officially authorized Report of the Commission of the German Constituent Assembly and of the

German Reichstag 1919-1928. Hoover War Library, 1934.

MCCLOSKY, HERBERT and TURNER, J. E. *The Soviet Dictatorship*. New York: McGraw-Hill, 1960. See chap. xvi "Regimentation of Thought and Culture," pp. 539-583.

MANVELL, ROGER. *Film*. (Revised Edition). Middlesex: Penguin Books, 1946, 237 pp. See especially Part II, "The Influence of the Film on Present-Day Society."

MANVELL, ROGER and FRAENKEL, HEINRICH. *Doctor Goebbels, His Life and Death*. London: Heinemann, 1960, 329 pp.

MARGOLIN, L. J. *Paper Bullets—A Brief Study of Psychological Warfare in World War II*. New York: Froben Press, 1946, 150 pp.

MARSHALL, JAMES *Swords and Symbols—The Techniques of Sovereignty*. New York Oxford University Press 1939, 163 pp.

MOCX, J. R. and LARSON, C. *Words That Won the War*. Princeton, New Jersey: University Press, 1939, 372 pp. The Story of the Committee on Public Information 1917-1919.

MOSCA, GAETANO. *Elementi di Scienza Politica*. Italy, 1896. English translation, *The Ruling Class*, by H. D. Kahn, Edited by A. Livingstone. New York and London: McGraw-Hill, 1939, 514 pp. See especially Chapters VI and VII.

NEUMANN, F. L. *Behemoth: The Structure and Practice of National Socialism*. New York: Oxford University Press, 1942, 532 pp.

ODEGARD, P. H. "Propaganda and Dictatorship," pp. 231-271 in G. S. FORD (ed.) *Dictatorship in the Modern World* (Second Edition). Minneapolis, Minnesota: University of Minnesota Press, 1939.

PARETO, VILFREDO. *Mind and Society*. Translated by A. LIVINGSTONE and A. BONGIORNO. New York: Harcourt, Brace, 1935. Sections 1747-1760 in Vol. III refer to propaganda.

PONSONBY, ARTHUR. *Falsehood in Wartime*. London: Allen and Unwin, 1928, 192 pp.

POUND, R. and HARMSWORTH, G. *Northcliffe*. London: Cassell, 1959, 933 pp.

READ, J. M. *Atrocity Propaganda 1914-1919*. New Haven, Connecticut: Yale University Press, 1941, 319 pp.

RIEGEL, O. W. *Mobilizing for Chaos, The Story of the New Propaganda*. New Haven, Connecticut: Yale University Press, 1934, 231 pp.

RUSSELL, BERTRAND. *Free Thought and Official Propaganda*. Conway Memorial Lecture, 1922. London: Watts, 1922, 48 pp.

———. *Power: A New Social Analysis*. London: Allen and Unwin, 1938, 328 pp. See especially Chapters ix "Power over Opinion," and Chapter x "Creeds as Sources of Power."

SAERCHINGER, *Cesar*. "Radio as a Political Instrument," *Foreign*

Affairs, XVI (1938), pp. 244-259.

SCHRAMM, WILBUR (ed.). *The Process and Effects of Mass Communication.* Urbana, Illinois: University of Illinois Press, 1955, 586 pp.

SCHUMAN, F. L. *The Nazi Dictatorship: A Study in the Social Pathology and the Politics of Fascism.* (Second revised edition). New York: Alfred A. Knopf, 1939, 516 pp.

SIMON, H. A. and STERN, F. "The Effects of Television Upon Voting Behavior in Iowa in the 1952 Presidential Election," *American Political Science Review,* IL (1955), pp. 470-477.

SINCLAIR, T. C. "The Nazi Party Rally at Nuremberg," *Public Opinion Quarterly,* II (1938), pp. 570-583.

SOREL, GEORGES. *Reflections on Violence.* Translated by T. E. Hulme. London: Allen and Unwin, 1915. Original edition, *Reflexions sur la Violence* published 1906.

SPEIER, H. "Psychological Warfare Reconsidered" in his *Social Order and the Risks of War.* New York: G. W. Stewart, 1952, pp. 433-455.

SQUIRES, J. D. *British Propaganda at Home and in the United States from 1914 to 1917* Cambridge, Massachusetts: Harvard University Press, 1935, 113 pp.

STEED, H. W. *Through Thirty Years 1892-1922.* (two vols). London: Heinemann, 1924, Vol. II describes the author's activities as a propagandist in World War I.

STUART, SIR CAMPBELL *Secrets of Crewe House.* London: Hodder and Stoughton, 1920, 240 pp.

SUMMERS, R. E. (ed.). *America's Weapons of Psychological Warfare.* The Reference Shelf 23(4). New York: H. W. Wilson, 1951, 206 pp. A series of readings describing modern propaganda techniques.

TABORSKY, EDUARD *Conformity Under Communism: A Study of Indoctrination Technique in East Europe.* Washington, D. C.: Public Affairs Press, 1958, 38 pp.

THE TIMES PUBLISHING CO. LTD. "British Propaganda in Enemy Countries," Chap. cccxiv in Vol. XXI of *The Times History and Encylopaedia of the War,* London: 1919.

TROTTER, WILFRED. *Instincts of the Herd in Peace and War.* London: Fisher Unwin, 1916, 264 pp.

UNITED STATES CONGRESS, HOUSE OF REPRESENTATIVES, COMMITTEE ON UN-AMERICAN ACTIVITIES. *Language as a Communist Weapon.* Consultation with Dr. Stefan T. Possony, 86th Congress, March 2, 1959, 53 pp.

——. *Communist Psychological Warfare (Brainwashing).* Consultation with Edward Hunter, 85th Congress, March 13, 1958, 26 pp.

UNITED STATES CONGRESS, SENATE, SUB-COMMITTEE ON THE JUDICIARY. *Brewing and Liquor Interests and German and*

Bolshevik Propaganda. (Three Vols.). 6th Congress, S. Res. 307 and 439 (1919).

——. *The Technique of Soviet Propaganda.* A Study Presented by the Sub-committee to Investigate the Administration of the Internal Security Act and Other Internal Security Laws of the Committee on the Judiciary, United States Senate. 86th Congress, 2nd Session. 1960, 38 pp.

WALLAS, GRAHAM. *The Great Society.* New York: Macmillan, 1914, 383 pp.

——. *Human Nature in Politics.* London: Constable, 1908, 302 pp.

WHITE, LLEWELLYN and LEIGH, R. D. *Peoples Speaking to Peoples, A Report on International Mass Communication from the Commission of Freedom of the Press.* Chicago, Illinois: University Press, 1946, 122 pp.

WOOLF, LEONARD. *Principia Politica: A Study of Communal Psychology.* London: Hogarth, 1953.

INDEX

150
3   2(2(
100

Printed in the USA
CPSIA information can be obtained
at www.ICGtesting.com
LVHW021151221023
761795LV00011B/636